HOSEA
THROUGH
MALACHI

WESLEY BIBLE STUDIES

wesleyan
PUBLISHING HOUSE
wphstore.com

CONTENTS

INTRODUCTION

The Cycle of Revival

It is easy to scoff at the ancient children of God and be amazed by their lack of commitment to a faithful God, but if we look honestly at ourselves and the times in which we live, we will see that the story hasn't changed much today. Even now, God's people repeat this cycle of unfaithfulness to the God who is always here, always patient, always ready to deliver us from the troubles of our own making. This familiar story is what makes the Minor Prophets so relevant to our relationship with God today. We can relate to a rebellious people.

While each prophet's message is nuanced by the particular circumstances of his day, one theme emerges from these writings that truly excites the imagination: God is the God of second chances. While He ruthlessly punishes sin, He always loves the sinner. He doesn't give up on us. Although He disciplines us, He is always ready to forgive.

In this study, you will explore three discoveries about God's judgment and mercy.

GOD JUDGES SIN

God offers extreme grace for the worst offenders. Yet this God of radical forgiveness is also radically intolerant of sin. He takes any sin among His holy people most seriously. It grieves His heart when His children rebel against Him, and it infuriates God to see the arrogance that fuels their rebellion.

God allows us to defy His will, but only for a while. Eventually, He will step in to bring judgment. The church today leans heavily on the grace of God, and rightly so—we can do nothing truly good without God. Yet there is a danger that this mind-set will lead first to arrogance and then to rebellion; we may use God's grace as a license to do as we please. The sinful abuse of this freedom can last only so long before God will act. The God of grace is also holy and just.

GOD WARNS HIS PEOPLE

Rarely does God bring judgment without warning. God offers a chance to repent—usually a second and third chance as well. This was the point of His sending prophets. Their task was to warn the people of impending doom and exhort them to repent. Sadly, the people rarely listened. Through these same prophets— as well as through the ministry of the Holy Spirit—God continues to urge His people to abandon selfish ways and be fully devoted to Him. God loves us enough to offer a second chance.

GOD RESTORES THE PENITENT

In ancient days, disaster was often the only thing that would break the hard hearts of God's people. Once softened, however, the people invariably turned back to God—their only true source of help. And God always responded in the same way: He loved them, forgave them, and restored them to a full relationship with himself. Though God punished His people, He never fully destroyed them. The fact that God responds to the penitent heart is completely inconsistent with other gods. Our all-powerful God is able to temper justice with mercy. He loves and forgives those who have wronged Him.

As you study the writings of these godly, passionate, often fiery-tongued preachers, allow their message to have the same effect on your heart that it did on many hearers of long ago—let it drive you back into the arms of the God who loves you.

1

THE GOD OF SECOND CHANCES

Hosea 1:2–11; 3:1–5

We belong to Christ first by creation, then by redemption.

Nearly everyone has experienced betrayal in some form. Dishonesty in a business partner, disloyalty in a teammate, infidelity in a spouse, abandonment by a parent—these are among the most painful human experiences. And they are not unique to people in our day or to those outside the church. God's people suffer these losses, too.

The story of Hosea is a story of betrayal. And it is a story of unrelenting love and unconditional forgiveness. But there is a twist. The story, real enough to Hosea and his family, was used by God as a parable to a wayward people. The patient husband is God. The wayward wife is God's people. Like an Old Testament version of the Prodigal Son, Hosea shows us the love of God through a graphic story of a broken family healed by grace.

What Hosea did—seeking out his unfaithful wife, finding her hopelessly enslaved, buying her back, bringing her home, loving her again—fills us with astonishment and admiration. When we realize that that is precisely what God has done for us, admiration gives way to adoration.

COMMENTARY

Hosea is positioned first among the twelve books of the Minor Prophets in the Old Testament. The book of Hosea is generally viewed by scholars as comprising two major divisions. The first three chapters present the object lesson that God gave to Hosea concerning his marriage to Gomer and their children, and its symbolism for Israel. The rest of the book is the message of God to Israel, a message of rebuke for their apostasy and a loving call to return.

Little is known about the prophet's background other than what we are told in 1:1. He is the son of the otherwise unknown Beeri. Even though Hosea ministered to the northern kingdom of Israel during the reign of Jeroboam II (782–753 BC), his ministry is dated by the span of four kings of the southern kingdom of Judah: Uzziah (767–740), Jotham (740–732), Ahaz (732–716), and Hezekiah (716–687). Since Assyria's annihilation of the northern kingdom occurred in stages between 734 and 721, the ministry of Hosea, according to 1:1, extended beyond the time of the ancient nation of Israel. Perhaps this indicates a possible reason for Hosea's frequent references to Judah (1:7, 11; 4:15; 6:11; 8:14; 12:2). The message of Hosea was the story of Israel's fall and call, told with hopes that the southern kingdom would heed its warnings.

This period of Israel's history, during the reign of Jeroboam II, was mixed. On the one hand it was a time of peace and economic prosperity. On the other hand, morally and spiritually the people's lives were corrupt and far from the God of their fathers.

An Object Lesson for Adulterous Israel (Hos. 1:2–11)

The ministry and message of Hosea begins with one of the most unusual passages in Scripture. The Lord directed His prophet to **"Go, take to yourself an adulterous wife and children of unfaithfulness, because the land is guilty of the vilest adultery in departing from the LORD"** (v. 2). Why would God tell Hosea, a prophet, to do such a thing? Scholars hold different views on this difficult question. Some would say Gomer was not immoral when Hosea married her, but God gave him knowledge that this woman would become unfaithful during the early days of their marriage and that this unfaithfulness would become a symbol of Israel's unfaithfulness to God. A second, less plausible, view is that the symbolism is merely literary and not a depiction of the real life of the prophet. At any rate, God is so passionately disturbed about the moral demise of His people that He resorts to strong measures to get their attention.

In obedience to the Lord's command, Hosea chose and **married Gomer daughter of Diblaim** (v. 3). There are eight references to the name Gomer in the Old Testament, half of which refer to the grandson of Noah through Japheth (Gen. 10:2–3; 1 Chron. 1:5–6), one to a group of people who descended from this son of Japheth (Ezek. 38:6), and the rest to Hosea's wife (Hos. 1:3, 6, 8). Some have attempted to assign significance to the meaning of her name, since the Hebrew root from which Gomer is derived can mean "to come to an end," "to complete," "to accomplish," or even "to perfect." But others have pointed to Hosea's practice of making clear the meaning of names when such is important to his message (1:4–9) and argued the absence of such for Gomer is indicative.

As for her race, ethnicity, or family heritage, the evidence is sparse. She is identified only as Diblaim's daughter, and this is the only occurrence of the name Diblaim in the Old Testament. However, there is no reason to believe Gomer was not a Jew. If she were not, certainly this detail would be mentioned, since God would be asking Hosea to intentionally break Jewish Law by marrying outside the faith.

Some have called her a prostitute, even suggesting she was a temple priestess. The KJV uses the word *harlot* to describe Gomer in 2:5. One cannot necessarily build a case for Gomer's harlotry on the appearance of this word alone. Unfaithfulness or adultery, certainly, but not necessarily for hire. However, other indicators would lend credibility to the KJV rendering. In the same verse (2:5) is the word "lovers," indicating a plurality of trysts. Also the verse says she is compensated well for her association with these men. Finally when Hosea wants her back, he has to buy her (3:2), which would indicate that her company goes for a price. While we cannot be dogmatic either way, we can understand the validity of both possibilities.

The children conceived by Gomer and said to be born to Hosea are each given names straight from the direction of the Lord with great significance. The first is a **son** (1:3) whose name, **Jezreel** (v. 4), is a reference to a very painful period in Israel's history. Mention of **the massacre at Jezreel,** for which God will mete out ultimate punishment—**"I will put an end to the kingdom of Israel"**—cites **the house of Jehu** as the guilty party (v. 4). God originally praised Jehu for taking vengeance against Ahab (2 Kings 10:30) after Ahab had basically stolen a vineyard in Jezreel from Naboth, its rightful owner, and had Naboth killed (1 Kings 21). After Ahab's death, Jehu having just been anointed king of Israel by Elisha (2 Kings 9), destroyed the evil Jezebel at Jezreel (2 Kings 9:30–33), and slaughtered all seventy members of the house of Ahab—anyone who may have been even remotely interested in succeeding their father (2 Kings 10). Finally he attempted to completely do away with Baal worship by shrewdly tricking all the ministers of Baal into gathering in one place, where he had them killed. Later prophetic statements indicate that this overzealous act by Jehu did not indicate his faithfulness to God, since Jehu did not follow that action by decisively turning away from the idolatrous practices of Jeroboam. As a result, God held him responsible for the subsequent defrauding of Israel (2 Kings 10:29). Because the Israelites followed Jehu in idolatry, God was ready to punish them by putting **an end to the kingdom of Israel** (Hos. 1:4). This **break** of **Israel's bow,** the military muscle they were currently enjoying, would take place **in the Valley of Jezreel** (v. 5). Israel was defeated in the battle of Jezreel by the Assyrian king Tiglath-Pileser III around 734 BC. That defeat led to the final overthrow of Israel.

The second child was a **daughter** named **Lo-Ruhamah,** meaning "unloved," because the Lord said, **"I will no longer show love to the house of Israel, that I should at all forgive them"** (v. 6). Hosea compared this rejection to God's abiding favor on **Judah** (v. 7), whom He would save by His own miracle-working power rather than by their military might of the **bow, sword or battle, or by horses and horsemen** (v. 7).

WORDS FROM WESLEY

Hosea 1:6

Lo-ruhamah—Not pitied. Israel's name had been through many ages Ruhamah, that is, pitied. God had pitied them, and saved them from their enemies. But now Israel should be no more pitied, God would throw them up to the rage of usurpers, and conspirators. (ENOT)

The third child is **another son** (v. 8). God told Hosea to name the boy **Lo-Ammi,** which means **not my people** (v. 9). The name was God's declaration of the abandonment of His unfaithful nation. But in His goodness, the Lord followed this prophecy with a reassurance of ultimate victory: **"Where it was said to them, 'You are not my people,' they will be called 'sons of the living God'"** (v. 10).

WORDS FROM WESLEY

Hosea 1:8

Loammi—That is, not my people. Tho' once you were a peculiar people, you are so no more; you are cast off as you deserved. *I will not be your God*—I will be a God to you, no more than to any of the heathen nations. This God executed when He gave them up into the hands of Salmaneser, who sent them were none now can find them. (ENOT)

The Redemption of Hosea's Wife and God's Redemption of Israel (Hos. 3:1–5)

Chapter 3 begins with God's command to Hosea: **"Go, show,"** meaning the divine initiative taken by Yahweh in seeking to save the unfaithful nation of Israel. This prophetic action by Hosea is a powerful symbol of the love of God that reaches a lost sinner. The key word here is *again*. This is a command to go a second time and give another chance to a woman who has caused deep wounds and scars in the home of the prophet.

The phrase **and love the sacred raisin cakes** of the NIV or the "flagons of wine" (v. 1) of the KJV both refer to the delicacies that tend to be served with idolatry.

Hosea's redemption of Gomer involves buying her back with his own money. This sacrificial love foreshadows the great love of God in sending His only Son to the the cross. The cost of Gomer's redemption is **fifteen shekels** [about six ounces] **of silver and a homer and a lethek of barley** [about ten bushels] (v. 2).

Hosea's renewed relationship with his wife included some stipulations. Hosea said to Gomer, **"You are to live with me many days; you must not be a prostitute or be intimate with any man, and I will live with you"** (v. 3).

The symbolism this marriage renewal carries for Israel is apparent. The **Israelites** after having gone **many days** without the primary elements of their political life (**king or prince**) or of their religious practice (**sacrifice, sacred stones, ephod, idol**) (v. 4) will find it good to **return and seek the LORD** (v. 5). Then they will fear the Lord (**come trembling**) and will experience **his blessings** once again.

Perhaps the key verse for this section is 2:23: "I will plant her for myself in the land; I will show my love to the one I called 'Not my loved one.' I will say to those called 'Not my people,' 'You are my people'; and they will say, 'You are my God.'" God reaches out to lost and hopeless sinners and redeems them, establishing them as part of His divine forever family, complete with all the benefits.

WORDS FROM WESLEY

Hosea 3:4

For—Now the parable is unfolded, it shall be with Israel as with such a woman, they and she were guilty of adultery, both punished long, both made slaves, kept hardly, and valued meanly, yet in mercy at last pardoned, and re-accepted tho' after a long time of probation. *Without a king*—None of their own royal line shall sit on the throne. *A prince*—Strangers shall be princes and governors over them. *Without a sacrifice*—Offered according to the law. *An image*—They could carry none of their images with them, and the Assyrians would not let them make new ones. *Ephod*—No priest as well as no ephod. *And without teraphim*—Idolatrous images kept in their private houses, like the Roman household gods; in one word, such should be the state of these captives they should have nothing of their own either in religious or civil affairs, but be wholly under the power of their conquering enemies. (ENOT)

DISCUSSION

If you are married, share the story of how you met your spouse. If you aren't married, share the story of how your parents met.

1. Why did God ask the prophet Hosea to marry an adulterous woman?

2. What other "object lessons" or enacted prophecies can you recall from the Old Testament?

3. Why do you think God chose to picture His relationship with His people as a marriage?

4. In what ways did "an adulterous wife and children of unfaithfulness" symbolize Israel?

5. In what way did Hosea symbolize God's persistent, unconditional love?

6. Despite God's love for His people, what consequences did Israel face for its unfaithfulness?

7. How does the image of God presented in this Scripture match contemporary conceptions of God in our culture?

8. In what ways is God tenderhearted in this Scripture, and in what ways is He stern? Do you see those characteristics in God today? How so?

9. How faithful are God's people today? In what ways might they be unfaithful?

PRAYER

Father, we have broken Your heart by our times of unfaithfulness. Our hearts are broken over our sin, and we humbly, but with great joy, receive Your offer of free and full forgiveness. Strengthen our resolve to never again violate our relationship with You.

2

A NEW BEGINNING

Joel 2:12–13, 21–32

If we return to God, He will restore us.

Joel delivered his prophecy to a people who had become prosperous and complacent. Distracted by the abundance of their lives, they had begun to ignore God. Their worship included the required sacrifices, but their lives were unchanged. Some had even strayed from the true faith and begun to worship idols. As they continued on this path, a national disaster occurred. An army of locusts swarmed into the land and decimated it, affecting the livestock as well as the agriculture. This devastation, Joel predicted, was but a foretaste of the coming judgment of God.

Yet the prophet's message is ultimately a message of hope: Whatever the locusts have destroyed, God is able to restore.

Today, we understand what it is to have our attention divided between God on the one hand and demanding careers, entertainment, and an abundance of possessions on the other. Joel's message couldn't be more timely. Disaster will come to those who ignore God; yet this same God is ready and willing to restore those who seek Him.

COMMENTARY

The book of Joel was written by a prophet of the same name. Joel means "Jehovah is God." He was a prophet to the southern kingdom (the tribes of Judah and Benjamin) during the period of the divided kingdom. Many believe he prophesied during the reign of Uzziah, around 800 BC.

As with many prophecies, Joel's includes a historical (present-day for Joel) as well as a far-reaching fulfillment. In this case, Joel speaks about the day of the Lord in three ways: as the terrible plague of locusts and accompanying drought the nation is experiencing, as the coming invasion of the Assyrians, and as a day in which God will take out His final judgment on the earth.

However, Joel's message is also one of joy. He looks forward to a day when the locust plague will come to an end and God will pour out rain on the land and it will once again produce crops. He also anticipates God's deliverance of Judah from the Assyrians, and he sees this outpouring of rain as a picture of the blessing of the Holy Spirit, which will precede the kingdom age.

Return to the Lord (Joel 2:12–13)

It often takes natural disasters for the Lord to get people's attention. In this case, God is calling out to the nation of Judah, which had turned away from Him and began to worship other gods, through a plague of locusts. In the midst of this calamity, He calls to them, **"Return to me with all your heart, with fasting and weeping and mourning"** (v. 12).

The priests generally called for only one fast per year—on the Day of Atonement (Lev. 16:29–31). However, according to Scripture, they could also call a fast in an emergency (see 2 Chron. 20:1–10). Note that this fast in Joel was called by God himself, not by the priests. Fasting in Scripture is a way of opening up the heart to the work of God. For example, we see both Moses and Jesus fasting for forty days in preparation for the work that God called them to do (see Ex. 34:28; Matt. 4:1–11).

In this instance, God was calling His people to return to Him not only by fasting, but also with weeping and mourning. The weeping and mourning represents a grieving over the sins they had committed. This was part of the repentance process. *Repentance* actually means "to change your mind." When we repent, we not only feel sorry about the sin, but we also have a desire to turn from the sin and go in another direction. Many times people only feel sorry that they were caught in their sin, rather than truly changing their mind to the extent that they no longer want to remain in their sin. When we genuinely repent, we have a change of mind and heart, and then begin to walk in a different direction.

WORDS FROM WESLEY

Joel 2:12

For it was not merely by the light of reason, or of natural conscience, as it is called, that the people of God have been, in all ages, directed to use fasting as a means to these ends; but they have been, from time to time, taught it of God himself, by clear and open revelations of his will. Such is that remarkable one by the prophet Joel: "Therefore saith the Lord, Turn ye to me with all your heart, and with fasting, and with weeping, and with mourning — Who knoweth if he will return and repent, and leave a blessing behind him? Blow the trumpet in Zion, sanctify a fast, call a solemn assembly — Then will the Lord be jealous for his land, and pity his people. Yea, I will send you corn, and wine, and oil — I will no more make you a reproach among the Heathen" (Joel 2:12). (WJW, vol. 5, 353)

The prophet told the people, **"Rend your heart and not your garments"** (Joel 2:13). The practice of fasting was often accompanied by outward signs such as disfiguring the face, lying on the ground and weeping, putting ashes on the head, wearing sackcloth, and tearing clothing. All these actions would bring attention to the fact that a person was fasting. God wasn't looking for outward signs; He was looking for inward changes. God was looking for those who genuinely were repenting of their sin. God will never reject those who truly repent by grieving over their sin and determining to change.

Today, God continually calls us to repentance. He calls us to turn from our sins and seek Him with hearts that are tender before Him—those that are broken and contrite. Fasting is not to be used to force God to do what we want, but to open our hearts to Him in a fresh way, so He can do His work there.

To do that, however, we must also have an understanding of who God is. Joel said God **is gracious and compassionate, slow to anger and abounding in love** (v. 13). In doing so, he told the nation not to fear, but to return to the Lord in confidence because of God's very loving and compassionate nature. We cannot repent just because we are afraid of the consequences of our sin. We must be convinced of God's love for us. Repentance is an act of love, not of fear.

Receive God's Blessing (Joel 2:21–27)

The locust plague in the previous verses was a picture of terror and destruction, an image of divine judgment on a nation that had fallen away from the Lord. But these next verses are an illustration of the great blessings that will come upon God's people when they repent.

Joel brought to mind pastures becoming green and trees bearing fruit. This is a stark contrast to the devastation of the locusts. He was saying that a time of harvest would return as God poured down His blessing upon those who genuinely repented.

WORDS FROM WESLEY

Joel 2:23

The former rain—The autumn rain which is needful to mellow the earth and fit it to receive the corn. *The latter rain*—Needful to bring forward and ripen the fruits, accounted the latter rain because these husbandmen and vine-dressers reckoned from seed time to spring and harvest. (ENOT)

He spoke of **abundant showers, both autumn and spring rains** (v. 23). We must realize that in the Holy Land, rain was (and is) a precious commodity and one of the most positive images available. The autumn rains generally occurred during October and November and were often called the early rain. These rains came at the time of the sowing of the seed and were needed to begin the germination process. The spring or latter rains occurred in March and April just before the harvest. These rains were needed in order to bring forth a bountiful harvest symbolized in this context as **threshing floors . . . filled with grain** and **vats** overflowing **with new wine and oil** (v. 24).

Joel was telling the people that God fulfills His promises. He was also showing God's people that God is faithful to bless us when we turn to Him in repentance. He said, **"You will have plenty to eat . . . and you will praise the name of the LORD your God, who has worked wonders for you"** (v. 26). God promises a time of blessing to those whose hearts are tender toward Him. And in turn, they will give praise and testimony of the Lord.

Be Filled with the Spirit (Joel 2:28–32)

Time phrases in Scripture are very important to note. Verse 28 begins with **and afterward**. After what? It would seem that this refers to a time after the plague of the locusts and after the coming Assyrian invasion. At that time, God promises not only to bless the land, but to **"pour out my Spirit on all people. . . . Even on my servants, both men and women I will pour out my Spirit in those days"** (vv. 28–29).

This is a prophecy about God generously giving His Spirit to *all* people. In the Old Testament, the Holy Spirit was not given to every believer, but came upon special people for specific tasks. And when those tasks were completed, the Holy Spirit would be removed from that life. The New Testament presents a much different experience beginning with the day of Pentecost.

Since then, every believer has the gift of the Holy Spirit at the moment we believe. We do not need to fear that the Spirit will be taken away when a special task is completed.

WORDS FROM WESLEY
Joel 2:28

Afterward—After the return out of Babylon, after the various troubles and salvations by which they may know that I am the Lord. *I will pour*—In extraordinary gifts on the first preachers of the gospel, and in various graces on all believers. *Upon all flesh*—Before these gifts were confined to one particular nation; but now they shall be enlarged to all nations, and all that believe. *Shall prophesy*—This was in part fulfilled according to the letter in the first days of the gospel; but the promise means farther, by pouring out of the spirit on your sons and your daughters, they shall have as full a knowledge of the mysteries of God's law, as prophets before-time had. *Shall dream dreams*—This also was literally fulfilled in the apostles days. But it may mean farther, the knowledge of God and His will shall abound among all ranks, sexes and ages in the Messiah's days, and not only equal, but surpass all that formerly was by prophesy, dreams, or visions. (ENOT)

As we examine the book of Acts, we see that the Holy Spirit was poured out only on Jews on the day of Pentecost. But as the church grew, both proselytes to the Jewish religion who were called "God fearers" and eventually Gentiles, would also receive this blessing. Truly God's promise to pour out His Spirit on *all* flesh—men and women, Jew and Gentile, slave and free—would be fulfilled.

We must realize that the "last days" began with the ministry of Jesus (Heb. 1:2) and will conclude on the day of the Lord. As we examine this passage, we see that its final fulfillment will be accompanied by miraculous signs in heaven and on earth: **"I will show wonders in the heavens and on the earth"** (Joel 2:30). Theses wonders will include seeing the **sun** turn **to darkness and**

the moon to blood before the coming of the . . . day of the
LORD (v. 31). We have begun to see strange natural wonders over
the past decades, but the wonders that will be seen at the end of
time will supersede anything we have ever seen.

And in that day **everyone who calls on the name of the LORD
will be saved** (v. 32). Paul quoted this verse in Romans 10:13 as
a promise to those who would open their hearts to the working
of the Holy Spirit. He is the One who draws the heart of an individual to God (John 6:44). Joel stated that **there will be deliverance . . . among the survivors whom the LORD calls** (Joel 2:32).
The day of the Lord will not only be a time of miraculous signs
in the heavens, but also a time of miraculous deliverance for those
who will trust in Him.

This Scripture reminds us that it is not our work that saves
us; it is the work of the Lord who calls us. We are called by the
Holy Spirit from sin and self to a living relationship with God
through Jesus Christ. This is a sovereign work of God. We
respond to Him because He takes the initiative. In 1 John 4:19,
we find these words: "We love because he first loved us."

God is calling unbelievers and believers alike into special fellowship with Him. We are called to turn away from the world's
philosophies, attitudes, and behaviors to do the work of Him who
loves us.

DISCUSSION

Share what comes to mind when you hear the word *prophet*.

1. The prophet Joel preached good news, but what is the prerequisite to it?

2. What do you think it means to return to the Lord "with all your heart"?

3. Describe a halfhearted believer.

4. Why do you think fasting is often mentioned as accompanying true repentance?

5. Joel instructed people, "Rend your heart and not your garments" (2:13). What do you think that means?

6. How would you define true repentance?

7. What are the "great things" God is promising?

8. God promises to "repay you for the years the locusts have eaten" (2:25), meaning that He will restore what has been lost. What have you lost? What have you seen God restore?

9. Does the church today need to repent? From what? Name some ways that could be accomplished.

PRAYER

Father, we live in a fallen world where we continue to experience some of the consequences of sin. But You have restored us to a place of honor in Your family, and Your blessings more than replace what was lost when we were away from You. Thank You for bringing us home.

（３）

THE ROAD TO RESTORATION

Amos 8:11–14; 9:8–15

Obedience is necessary for
maintaining a relationship with God.

God made an agreement with the children of Israel: He would be their God and they would be His people, representing Him to the rest of the world. Both parties had responsibilities in this agreement. Additionally, there were consequences to breaking the agreement. Such an agreement is known as a covenant.

God chose the Israelites to be a covenant people. This study reminds us of our agreement with God, and about how seriously God takes that agreement. God has chosen to enter into a covenant with humanity. If we choose to accept this agreement, obedience is required. The consequence to disobedience is judgment while the reward of obedience is blessing. God is compassionate and full of mercy, providing second chances when we fail. Obedience is a goal that must continually be sought.

COMMENTARY

Sandwiched among the twelve Minor Prophets is the prophet Amos. Amos 1:1 tells us he was "one of the shepherds of Tekoa"—a village in the hill region about twelve miles south of Jerusalem. Amos appears to have been more than a mere shepherd; the word describing him here is a "breeder of sheep"—one who evidently must have possessed large herds and had skill at managing and strengthening those herds. Amos 7:14 also describes him as a farmer who "took care of sycamore-fig trees." Sycamore-figs are large trees found in the fertile lowlands of the Jordan River and around the Dead Sea. Three or four times each year they bear a fig-like fruit. The sweetness of the fruit is enhanced when it is slit or scratched during the growing process. So Amos's occupation was as "fruit slitter" as well as a sheep breeder.

Amos made a point of his occupation when he was confronted by Amaziah, a local priest of the calf-god in Bethel in 7:14–15. He pointedly says to Amaziah, "I was neither a prophet, nor a prophet's son . . . but the LORD . . . said to me, 'Go, prophesy to my people Israel.'"

Even the name Amos means "burden" or "burden bearer." It is doubtful that as Amos was breeding sheep back in Tekoa, he thought he would be called by God to be His messenger. But nonetheless, Amos obeyed and delivered a stern message of warning and hope to Israel.

On the minor-prophet timeline Amos was probably one of the earliest of the prophets, his ministry dating around 760–750 BC. After King Solomon died, the kingdom of Israel was split into two parts—the period of the divided kingdom. The southern portion of the kingdom contained the tribes of Judah and Benjamin (known as Judah), and the remaining ten northern tribes were considered the northern kingdom (known as Israel). Samaria was the capital of Israel—which would later fall to Assyria in 722 BC; and Jerusalem was the capital of Judah—which would fall to Babylon in 586 BC.

Amos was a resident of Tekoa in Judah—the southern kingdom; but his message was to Bethel in Israel, the northern kingdom. As a shepherd, Amos made regular trips to the northern city of Bethel (about twelve miles north of Jerusalem) to sell his wool. During these trips, he had ample time to see the various activities of the city of Bethel.

Bethel was a wicked place to live. King Jeroboam had built a golden calf in the city to worship. The pleasures of worship around this golden calf were displeasing to God and destructive to the people of the city. As we read through Amos, not only do we see that the book is full of illustrations of idolatry, immorality, and wanton luxury, but this behavior is practiced at the expense of the poor, who are abused and unjustly treated (see 2:6–7; 4:1; 5:11–12; 8:4–6). It would be fair to say that this ungodly behavior broke the heart of Amos. So when the call of God came to him to prophesy in Bethel, Amos already knew firsthand the ungodliness of the people and the challenge that lay before him.

Amos did not compromise in proclaiming the message he was given by the Lord. But he judiciously began by describing the judgment God intended to bring on the neighboring cities and regions to Bethel. Beginning with Damascus, then Gaza, Tyre, Edom, Ammon, Moab, and the southern kingdom Judah, Amos boldly declared the impending destruction. Time after time, the "fire" of the Lord will "consume the fortresses" of these surrounding cities (1:4, 7, 10, 12, 14; 2:2, 5).

One can imagine the listening crowd affirming Amos's words. But then the hammer drops close to home in 2:6: "This is what the LORD says: 'For three sins of Israel, even for four, I will not turn back my wrath.'" Destruction will come to the city of Bethel and the house of Israel.

Amos executed the Lord's message starting far from Bethel in the city of Damascus, and zeroing-in like a hawk circling for the kill until the message of destruction fell on the city of Bethel and its people. (Note these cities and the progression of Amos's prophecy on a map of the divided kingdom.)

Chapters 3–6 then describe the nature of the expected destruction. But for God this is not simply a matter of vengeance. It is a call for justice anchored in God's response to hypocrisy in His people (see 5:21–24). Why did God "despise" their "religious festivals" and their worship (5:21)? Because their worship and lifestyle were not consistent. The people say one thing in worship and do something totally contrary the next day. God's response was reasonable: "Justice [will] roll on like a river, righteousness like a never-failing stream!" (5:24). And it will be executed with a price to the disobedient: "exile beyond Damascus" into Assyria (5:27).

Then in chapters 7–9 Amos described five visions of what would happen as God executed this justice. Visions of "swarms of locust" that would strip "the land clean" (7:1–2); "judgment by fire" that would devour the land (7:4); a "plumb line" (7:7) of morality that found Israel wanting; a "basket of ripe fruit" revealing the time has come (8:2); and finally the "altar" of the Lord at which judgment occurs (9:1).

The Death of the Word of God (Amos 8:11–14)

Perhaps the saddest part of the Lord's judgment is upon the people's obstinate attitude toward the Word of God recorded in 8:11–14. The hypocrisy of their religion leads the people to the point of a complete **famine of hearing the words of the LORD** (v. 11). Their ears have become deaf to what God has to say to them. Repeatedly in Israel's history, and now through the prophet Amos, God pleaded with His people, "Seek me and live" (5:4), and "Seek good, not evil" (5:14), yet the people ignored the cry of their Lord. Now, they searched **for the word of the LORD, but they will not find it** (8:12). It is not found because their callous hearts continually rejected its message, and **famine of hearing** (v. 11) was the end result. They neglected God's message so long that they could no longer hear Him. Despite their search for respite, for explanation, for forgiveness, for relief from their stubbornness, they did not find it. So dedicated are they to worshiping the gods of **Dan** and **Beersheba** (v. 14), God was unable to satisfy their spiritual hunger and thirst.

The church has embraced the Word of God—God's revelation of himself to His people—as life-giving and sustaining. Yet, how is God's Word treated in our worship today? Is it read? Is it expounded? Do we study it in our homes and private times? Will we experience a famine from God's Word because we are distracted in our worship and busy lives?

Amos painted a bleak picture for the people of Israel because of their sin and the inevitability of God's justice. Could God really forgive these people? Would He? Or to make it a bit more personal—will God really forgive a terrible sinner?

Restoration for the Hopeless (Amos 9:8–15)

Certainly justice will come from the **Sovereign Lord . . . on the sinful kingdom. He will destroy it from the face of the earth** (v. 8). There appears to be no mercy here. Obliteration seems to be the end result. **Yet He will not totally destroy the house of Jacob** (v. 8). Despite their disobedience, the people of God still have hope.

The house of Israel will be **shaken** just **as grain is shaken in a sieve** (v. 9). As grain is separated from the chaff, the chaff is blown away by the wind, and the heavier good grain falls to the ground. The chaff will blow away—there is no escape. **"All**

the sinners among my people will die by the sword" (v. 10). Their hypocrisy will bring them to certain ruin. But this process also identifies and separates out the good grain that remains.

WORDS FROM WESLEY

Amos 9:9

The least grain—Though tumbled and tossed with the great violence, yet the smallest, good grain, shall not be lost or destroyed. (ENOT)

"In that day I will restore David's fallen tent" (v. 11). Restoration will be through the seed of David, whose kingdom will rule forever (2 Sam. 7). And from David's seed **all the nations** will **bear my name** (Amos 9:12). The Genesis 15 promise to Abraham continues, and from his line all nations will be blessed. God's people Israel "only have I chosen of all the families of the earth" (Amos 3:2).

God's greatest promise is **"I will bring back my exiled people Israel"** (9:14). The people of God will be home from exile **in their own land, never again to be uprooted** (v. 15). The **ruined cities** will be rebuilt, the **vineyards** will be replanted, and the **gardens** will yield **fruit** (v. 14). Once again God's people, those who remain faithful and obedient through the judgment, will find the land of promise.

WORDS FROM WESLEY

Amos 9:15

Behold the days come—Here is another promise literally of abundant plenty to the returned captives, and mystically of abundant grace poured forth in gospel-days. *The plowman*—Who breaks up the ground, and prepares it for sowing, shall be ready to tread on the heels of the reaper who shall have a harvest so large, that before he can gather it all in, it shall be time to plow the ground again. *The treader of grapes*—So great shall their vintage be that e'er the treaders of grapes can have finished their work, the seeds-man shall be sowing his seed against the next season. *Shall drop*—The vineyards shall be so fruitful, and new wine so plentiful as if it ran down from the mountains. *Shall melt*—Or as if whole hills were melted into such liquors. If any object, it never was so: I answer, the sins of the returned captives prevented these blessings, which are promised under a tacit condition. (ENOT)

Amos unquestionably was looking into the future in these closing verses. In retrospect we see the agent of restoration found in the person of Jesus Christ, the Son of David's line, born in Bethlehem. **The days are coming** (v. 13) when a complete restoration for *all* God's people will occur. In that day **the reaper will be overtaken by the plowman**—the harvest will be so great that the one plowing will catch up to the harvester. **And the planter** will be found on the heels of **the one treading grapes**. The lushness of the grapes **will drip from the mountains and flow from all the hills** (v. 13). Certainly these metaphors describe the bounty of the restored land; however, they are also snapshots of the future restored kingdom of God's people.

This promise of restoration from exile is also for the believer today. The kingdom of Jesus Christ is *now*. It has begun. Certainly it is not complete; there is still trouble in this fallen world. But today, as believers in the salvation of Jesus Christ, we are participants in this new kingdom. The blessings of the kingdom are not solely for some far-off future time, but for the fellowship of believers today.

WORDS FROM WESLEY

Amos 9:15

Pulled up—On condition that they seek the Lord. This was on God's part with admirable constancy performed through six hundred years, perhaps the longest time of freedom from captivity they ever knew. (ENOT)

God's people Israel were destined to represent God to all people—the whole seed of Abraham. They were chosen by God as ambassadors to the pagan world. And today, as Gentiles, we are participants in the blessings of the kingdom of Jesus Christ. (Read Acts 15 to see this discussion in the early Jerusalem council.)

The result of participation in God's kingdom is boundless blessing and prosperity (Amos 9:13–15). Not wealth for wealth's sake, but God's blessing upon all His faithful people, regardless of race, ethnicity, gender, or socioeconomic class. God calls His people to himself to inherit the bounty of His kingdom.

God's restoration is for today but comes on the heels of a better blessing tomorrow. Today we are still strangers, foreigners, and exiles in a strange land. This is not our home, but we are intended to dwell with God for eternity. It is our responsibility now to prepare for that complete restoration. It is difficult to understand why some Christians carelessly live like the Devil and somehow expect God to reform them as they enter the pearly gates. God calls us to live *today* like Christians—His holy people—so that we might be ready for eternity with Him.

DISCUSSION

Share your experiences with famine or the hungry: volunteering at a soup kitchen, feeding the homeless, helping the hungry on a mission trip, etc. Share what impacted you the most.

1. Amos prophesized about a famine, but not a famine of food or water. He was talking about an absence of God's Word. How could such a famine occur?

2. Using Amos's metaphor of famine, how would you say the church is doing today regarding Scripture: full and feasting, lean and healthy, underfed and hungry, starving to death?

3. What causes people to ignore God's Word? What whets their appetite for it?

4. Spirituality is a popular topic in today's culture. Do you sense that this is a genuine hunger for God? Why or why not?

5. How are today's seekers attempting to satisfy that hunger?

6. During this prophecy, God abruptly shifted His attention to pronounce judgment. Why?

7. Do you think this prophecy was intended only for the people of the ancient world, or might it apply to others? To us?

8. What do you think it means that "David's tent" has fallen? How could that situation be corrected?

9. What could we do to better feed ourselves on the Word of God?

10. What do you think would be the result if there was a revival of Bible knowledge in today's church? How might that come to pass?

PRAYER

Father, we want our worship to be acceptable to You because it is accompanied by a lifestyle that is approved by You. Purify our hearts by Your Holy Spirit, and make us people who hate evil, love good, and seek justice for all people.

4

RECLAIMING GOD'S INHERITANCE

Obadiah 1–4, 15–21

God has planned the restoration of His wayward people.

Obadiah is the shortest book in the Old Testament, and it carries a strong message of judgment and destruction. Unlike many other prophets, Obadiah offers no hope and no second chances. The Edomites had sinned against God. Their pride caused them to believe that they were untouchable, and no one, not even God, could conquer them. They were wrong.

This is the "problem" with God's grace; if not properly understood, it can lead to arrogance and complacency. God's eagerness to forgive can lead us to believe that He does not abhor sin. He does. God's incredible patience might cause us to think that there will always be more time to set our lives in order. There won't. The abundance of God's blessings may create the impression that we ourselves have unlimited resources and power. We don't.

The purpose of Obadiah's prophecy was to announce the destruction of Edom because of her pride and sin against Judah. Today's study stands as a stark reminder that God's grace, though freely available, must not be taken for granted. The day of the Lord will finally come.

COMMENTARY

In this book, the prophet Obadiah was not focusing on Judah and Israel, but on Edom's sin and the coming judgment. This is another chapter in the struggle that began with Jacob and Esau while they were still in the womb and continued between their descendants, the Edomites and the Israelites. Remember that Esau settled in the area of Mount Seir, and the people who lived there (Horites) became part of his people. The Edomites wouldn't allow the Israelites to pass through their land when they came out of Egypt. Obadiah dealt with the sin and pride of the Edomites and prophesies their complete annihilation. He didn't close on that negative note, though. He gave prophecy for the restoration of Israel as God's favored people and ended with a promise that exists for us today: "And the kingdom will be the LORD's" (v. 21).

Obadiah's Vision of Retribution: Judgment against Edom (Obad. 1–4)

Obadiah began by identifying himself as a messenger and envoy of the Lord, who is Yahweh: **An envoy was sent to the nations to say . . .** (v. 1). He was calling the nations to prepare for battle against the Edomites. Their reign of intimidation, arrogance, and pride was coming to an end.

The name Obadiah means "worshiper" or "servant of God." There are two periods in Israel's history that may date this prophet. The first is the invasion of Jerusalem by Philistines and Arabs during the reign of Jehoram (853–841 BC). In this time frame, he was probably a contemporary of Elisha. The other is the Babylonian attacks on Jerusalem (605–586 BC). In this era, he would have been a contemporary of Jeremiah. Obadiah may have thought the conspiracy among Arab tribes against Edom was the action of God. He was an ambassador telling the people that God was going to bring nations against Edom in battle. His prophecy is an echo of Jeremiah 49:14: "I have heard a message from the LORD: An envoy was sent to the nations to say, 'Assemble yourselves to attack it! Rise up for battle!'"

WORDS FROM WESLEY
Obadiah 1

Obadiah—His name speaks a servant or a worshiper of the Lord, but who he was we know not. *We*—The prophets, have heard. *A rumour*—Not an uncertain report, but it comes from God. *Is sent*—By the Lord first, and next by Nebuchadnezzar who executed on Edom what is here foretold. *The nations*—Those that were confederate with, or subject to Nebuchadnezzar. (ENOT)

The Lord said, **"I will make you small among the nations"** (Obad. 2). The Edomites were a proud people who thought no one could conquer them. At five thousand feet above sea level, they felt that their country was impenetrable. But God said, **"The pride of your heart has deceived you"** (v. 3). They had come to depend on their own knowledge and strength. **"From there I will bring you down"** (v. 4). As a result of this, Edom would be made small, become despised, and cease to exist. In other words, God was going to cut them down to size!

Lebanon and Syria are where Israel (Jacob) and his family settled. Jordon is where Edom (Esau) and his descendents were established. Edom was a country carved into the rock. The capital was Sela, later called Petra. Both words mean rock. The location is about fifty miles south of the southern end of the Red Sea. It was a poor area, only accessible by a mile-long canyon. Their homes were carved into the rock of the mountains (v. 3), and the Edomites felt they were invincible because of their location. Obadiah compared them to the **eagle** (v. 4), which soars high and proud, building its nest in high places. Pride is a result of fallen human nature, causing us to exalt ourselves rather than the Creator. Sometimes we who have the least reason for pride have the most of it, and are guilty of the Edomites' sin. The truth is, however, God can bring us down at any time.

WORDS FROM WESLEY
Obadiah 4

Bring thee down—God who is in the heavens would throw thee down. When men could not marshal armies against thee, stars should fight in their courses against thee. Nothing can stand which God will cast down (Jer. 49:16–17). (ENOT)

Restoration: Judgment versus Justice (Obad. 15–17)

Verse 15 contains a foreshadowing of judgment day: **The day of the LORD is near for all nations.** God will exact retribution upon Edom for their sins against Judah. He was also saying that the same distress and calamity that befell Judah was near for them. Everything the Edomites had done to other nations would be done to them. The Edomites cursed Israel, so they were cursed. **"As you have done, it will be done to you"** (v. 15) becomes Edom's curse. But what about the rest of the nations? They were not all dealt with at that time.

"Just as you drank on my holy hill, so all the nations will drink continually" (v. 16). The Israelites' bitter cup was temporary, but Edom's troubles would result in complete destruction.

Obadiah's message is an Old Testament illustration of a New Testament principle: "Do to others as you would have them do to you" (Luke 6:31). We go to God asking for His mercy, but very often fail to extend it to others. If we want to be blessed, then we have to extend blessings to others. Obadiah said nations will drink the bitter potion of God's judgment and be swallowed up in destruction. This would be a total vindication for Judah, because Edom, and all of Esau's descendents, would be completely destroyed. There were no pleas to return and no words of hope or consolation. However, just as there would be destruction for Edom, God promised salvation for Israel. God would use Israel to bring judgment against Edom.

Verse 17—**But on Mount Zion will be deliverance**—is the hope for Israel. We see two eschatological references here: judgment on God's enemies and blessings on God's people. In this verse, Obadiah alluded to the coming deliverance and Israel's second chance and mentions three promises:

1. There will be deliverance.
2. There will be holiness.
3. Israel's **house of Jacob will possess its inheritance** (v. 17).

The Israelites had a Promised Land, but they were not always in possession of it. Sometimes they occupied it without owning it. As long as the children of Jacob were in bondage and they were not delivered, they could not possess their inheritance. Today there are many who are in bondage to their possessions and need deliverance. We cannot take possession of all that God has for us until we are delivered from sin, pride, and anything else that has ownership of our hearts.

WORDS FROM WESLEY
Obadiah 17

Zion—Literally this refers to the Jews: typically to the gospelchurch. *Deliverance*—A remnant that shall be delivered by Cyrus, a type of Israel's redemption by Christ. *Holiness*—The temple, the city, the people returned from captivity shall be holy, to the Lord. *Their possessions*—Their own ancient possessions. (ENOT)

Promise of Redemption (Obad. 18–21)

The house of Joseph will be **a flame; the house of Esau will be stubble. . . . There will be no survivors from the house of Esau** (v. 18). God had said earlier that He would destroy Edom using Israel. Now the prophecy from Obadiah was that it will be done with other nations, and there will be no survivors. The immediate meaning is that the trials and burdens of the Israelites, who are God's chosen people, are only temporary. Judah will be restored and all Israel will be delivered. The attack against Edom is very different. Israel **will be a fire,** and Edom **will be stubble** and will be completely devoured (v. 18). God's word given through Obadiah proved true. The Edomites fought side by side with the Jews during the rebellion against Rome in AD 66–70 and were crushed by Rome. The Edomites were never heard of as a people again.

WORDS FROM WESLEY

Obadiah 19

They—The Jews who live in the south parts of Canaan, next Idumea, shall after their return and victories over Edom, possess his country. *Of the plain*—The Jews who dwell in the plain country, shall enlarge their borders, possess the Philistines country, together with their ancient inheritance. The former was fully accomplished by Hyrcanus. And if this were the time of fulfilling the one, doubtless it was the time of fulfilling the other also. And all the land which the ten tribes possessed, shall again be possessed by the Jews. *Gilead*—Here is promised a larger possession than ever they had before the captivity; and it does, no doubt, point out the enlargement of the church of Christ in the times of the gospel. (ENOT)

In the judgment against Edom, we also see a second chance for Israel. The coming deliverance will allow the Israelites to occupy and possess the land that once belonged to Esau. **People from the Negev** (v. 19) refers to those living in the dry wasteland area in the south. All this land in and around Israel will be occupied by God's chosen people. **People from the foothills** (v. 19) is another reference to the Israelites and shows the territory that will be returned to them. **The land of the Philistines** (v. 19) refers to the Mediterranean coast, west of Judah. They will also possess **Ephraim**, **Samaria**, **Gilead**, **Zarephath**, and the **Negev** (vv. 19–20). The mention of **Benjamin** (v. 19) may indicate that the area is to be divided among the ten tribes.

Even though the modern borders of Israel do not encompass the ancient lands of Edom, we can trust that one day they will, either in this age or the age to come. There were "saviors," or **deliverers** (v. 21), for Israel (v. 21) and destruction for Edom. The deliverers came to judge the **mountains of Esau** in three ways:

- The presence of the deliverers was a judgment against Edom.
- The judges would rule over the territory of Edom.
- The judges would sit in judgment over Edom for their sins.

There was justice for Israel and redemption through the deliverers.

And the kingdom will be the LORD's (v. 21). This is the victory for Israel, as prophesied by Obadiah, and the central theme of encouragement for God's people. Mount Zion will be exalted over the mountains of Esau. The broader reference is to the Lord and His ultimate rule over all nations and all of creation. Jesus Christ came to be the ultimate Savior for us all.

Why is this blood feud between Jacob and Esau repeatedly addressed in the Bible? It shows God's ongoing protection of His people from their enemies. It also demonstrates to us that God's standards extend beyond His chosen people. Every nation will be judged by its own standard, just like Edom. Revelation 11:15 says, "The kingdom of the world has become the kingdom of our Lord and of his Christ, and he will reign for ever and ever." Regardless of the temporary difficulties we may face today, Obadiah's promise that the kingdom will be the Lord's is our hope.

DISCUSSION

Discuss what the nations of today rely on.

1. Do you think God has been involved in governmental affairs throughout history? If so, name some examples.

2. Why did God cause the nations to rise up against Edom? Do you think He would cause a similar uprising of nations today? Why? Against whom?

3. God seems to take particular offense at the sin of pride. How was Edom prideful? How are nations today prideful? How are we?

4. What do individuals rely on for a sense of power and protection? What do you rely on?

5. What Scriptures come to mind that are similar to Obadiah 15?

6. Name the principle and the warning that God gives to those who are proud, self-absorbed, and use their superior advantages to disadvantage others. To whom might this principle and warning apply today? Might they apply to you?

7. Based on Obadiah's prophecy, what message would you give to the political leaders in your nation?

PRAYER

Father, we have so many good things in our lives, and we count them as blessings from Your hand. May we never become so comfortable living with these blessings that we believe we have earned them or gained them on our own, turning them from blessings into curses.

5

SAVED BY GRACE

Jonah 1:1–5, 11–17; 2:1, 10; 3:1–2, 10; 4:9–11

Salvation is based on God's mercy, not human merit.

Who do you least want to see in heaven? If we are honest with ourselves, we can likely offer some answer to that question. Those who make war on our country deserve justice not mercy, right? Anyone who abuses a helpless child should have no place in God's house, correct? Terrorists. Pedophiles. Murderers. These people don't *deserve* God's grace, isn't that true?

In fact, none of us deserve God's grace. While it is true that some acts are particularly shocking and loathsome, there is no one whom God doesn't love and want to see redeemed. His grace is for everyone. That's the message of the book of Jonah.

Children can easily recite the story of Jonah, the prophet who ran from God's will, was pitched overboard in a storm, and was swallowed by a big fish. Most of us, however, stop recounting the story at the point when Jonah was spat up on dry land. But that is really the beginning of the story. We go on to see the prophet's petty motive for refusing to offer salvation and his petulant insistence that God should destroy the Ninevites—even *after* they repented!

To a world that insists on labeling people as either "us" or "them," this study issues a necessary reminder that no one deserves salvation—it is God's gift to all who will humble themselves and call on Him.

COMMENTARY

Jonah is unique among the Minor Prophets; it is the narrative of a single extended episode in the life of the prophet for whom it is named. It contains a single prophetic oracle—only five words in the Hebrew text. Even the poetry comprising most of chapter 2 is Jonah's personal prayer, not an oracle.

The only other Old Testament mention of Jonah is 2 Kings 14:25, a report that Jeroboam II, the last strong king of Israel, restored the northern kingdom briefly to its former greatness, as Jonah had prophesied. Jeroboam II reigned about 793–753 BC; this would place Jonah's prophecy perhaps about 780 BC. From 2 Kings 14:25 we learn also that Jonah was from Gath Hepher in the hills of lower Galilee, not far from the later Nazareth. Thus, Jonah was an Israelite, not a Judean like most of the prophets.

As we shall see in this study, the message of this book is that God loves all people and does not desire that any should perish. Whether Jonah (or we) care to see it or not, God extends grace not just to (imperfect) believers like Jonah (and us), but even to pagan sailors and national "enemies" like Nineveh. God is the God of grace to all.

Jonah Tried to Flee from God (Jon. 1:1–5)

The word of the LORD came (v. 1) is a common introduction to prophetic oracles, even to a prophetic book. **Jonah** means "dove"; **Amittai** may mean "Yahweh is faithful."

God's command began with the verb **go** (v. 2), again, a common way of beginning instructions to God's agents, the prophets. **Nineveh**, capital of the Assyrian Empire, lay on the east bank of the upper Tigris River, about five hundred miles northeast of Samaria, Israel's capital. By road, it was about seven hundred miles, a fifty-day journey on foot.

Three locations in the Mediterranean were named **Tarshish** (v. 3); one was the port city in south-central Anatolia (Turkey) known in New Testament times as Tarsus. The other two were in the western Mediterranean, one on the island of Sardinia, the second, Tartessos, in Spain. Whichever one Jonah hoped to reach, we may wonder how he thought he could escape God by fleeing westward, knowing already that God's knowledge and interest extended far beyond Israel!

WORDS FROM WESLEY
Jonah 1:3

From the presence—From the place where God usually had shewed himself present, by revealing His word and will to His prophets. Perhaps he might think God would not put him upon this work, when he was in a strange country. (ENOT)

The Hebrew writer clearly intended to make the point that to flee from God is to go down. The text is vivid: **He** [Jonah] ***went down* to Joppa** (v. 3, emphasis added), and later he "had *gone down* into the hold of the ship" (v. 5 NRSV, emphasis added). Though the verb is not present in verse 15, it is clear the sailors threw Jonah down into the sea, and his prayer from the fish's belly includes his report, "To the roots of the mountains I *sank down*" (2:6, emphasis added). One cannot escape God's reach; one only can reach the depths trying.

Sailors (1:5) is from the same root as the Hebrew noun for "salt"; we are justified in thinking of the English phrase "old salts." **Each cried out to his own god** (v. 5). They were probably all pagans.

The sailors not only prayed; they acted: **They threw the cargo into the sea to lighten the ship** (v. 5). This **threw** is the same verb used to describe God sending **a great wind upon the sea** (v. 4). More easily than the sailors heaving the cargo overboard, God took a wind from God's "storm cupboard" (see Job 38:22–24) and tossed it upon the sea to stop Jonah from reaching Tarshish.

Pagan Sailors Responded to God (Jon. 1:11–16)

Meanwhile, the captain discovered Jonah sleeping below deck, probably as they moved cargo topside. He awoke Jonah, the crew pressed him to identify himself, and he admitted to running away from Yahweh, whom he identified as the One **who made the sea and the land** (v. 9). More terrified than ever, they asked Jonah what he had done. The author's note, **the sea was getting rougher and rougher** (v. 11), implies they didn't wait for Jonah's answer, but cut to their next question: **"What should we do to you?"** (v. 11). Jonah's act threatened their lives; Jonah should know how they could escape.

Jonah's reply, **"Pick me up and throw me into the sea"** (v. 12), was his only heroic act in the entire story. One could argue even this was not heroic, as Jonah must have assumed he would die either way. Moreover, Jonah probably believed, with many of his place and time, that if he were not buried after his death, his spirit would wander until the end of time. Offering himself for that fate, on behalf of the sailors, we *may* see as heroism.

Finding it impossible to reach the shore, the sailors prayed again, but this time, to Jonah's God, Yahweh. They knew they had to throw Jonah overboard, and they knew that could be seen as murder. They appealed to Yahweh's understanding of their hearts, which they may not have thought possible before this, and to Yahweh's sovereign will, incomprehensible to them in this extremity. A legitimate translation of the last part of their prayer is, "For You are Yahweh; just as you have delighted to do, you have done."

Then they took Jonah and threw him overboard, and the raging sea grew calm (v. 15). Here again, **threw** is the same

Hebrew verb used of God sending the wind (v. 4) and of the sailors throwing the cargo overboard (v. 5). Jonah may not have weighed more than the clay jars, but it certainly would have been more difficult for them to force themselves to throw him into the raging sea. Yet, as soon as Jonah disappeared, the sea stood calm.

Then the men feared Yahweh, a great fear, and they sacrificed sacrifices and vowed vows. Three times, the verb and the direct object are from the same root; this usage strengthens a statement. Also, this is the fear and reverence of God enjoined all through the Bible. Finally, while anyone *could* be merely grateful and "sacrifice sacrifices," these men also "vowed vows." Vows are for the future. We cannot be sure these pagan sailors went on to worship only Yahweh, but they did, at least, worship Him along with their other gods. For their time and place (and perhaps until they could learn more about Yahweh), we may speak of this as the conversion of these "old salts."

WORDS FROM WESLEY

Jonah 1:16

Feared the Lord—Perhaps as Jonah's casting over-board was a type of Christ's death, so the effect it had upon the mariners might be a type of the conversion of the heathen from idols unto God. *Made vows*—Probably they vowed, they would ever worship Him whom Jonah preached, the Creator of heaven and earth. (ENOT)

God Rescued Jonah (Jon. 1:17—2:1, 10)

Meanwhile, what of Jonah? God **provided a great fish** (1:17); there's that word **great**, again, and it was a fish, not a whale. The Hebrew is clear on that point.

From inside the fish Jonah prayed (2:1); it would be easy to assume this was Jonah's request for God to deliver him from the fish. Reading the prayer, however, makes clear that it was not. This is a prayer of thanksgiving to God for already saving Jonah from death. As soon as he realized he had been swallowed, yet still could breathe, Jonah knew God was using the fish to save his life. Sure enough, when Jonah had three days to think, the fish came close to shore, and **vomited Jonah onto dry land** (2:10).

Pagan Nineveh Responded to God (Jon. 3:1–2, 10)

Then the word of the LORD came to Jonah (v. 1); this is five words in Hebrew, the same five words, exactly, that begin the book in 1:1. The difference follows in the next phrase (one word in Hebrew): **a second time** (3:1). The God of the Bible, the God of Israel, the God revealed in Christ, is the God of second chances. God could have let Jonah drown and called another prophet; Israel had many in those days. God wanted Jonah to deliver this message to Nineveh, however, so God extended Jonah's life and gave him a second chance.

WORDS FROM WESLEY

Jonah 3:2

Exceeding great—The greatest city of the known world at that day, it was then in its flourishing state greater than Babylon, whose compass was three hundred eighty-five furlongs, but Nineveh was in compass four hundred and eighty. It is said, her walls were a hundred foot in height, her walls broad enough for three coaches to meet, and safely pass by each other; that it had fifteen hundred towers on its walls, each two hundred foot high, and one million, four hundred thousand men employed for eight years to build it. *Of three days journey*—To walk round the walls, allowing twenty miles to each day's journey. (ENOT, Jon. 3:3)

We discover in chapter 4 that, despite this, Jonah still did not approve of giving Nineveh and its people a second chance. We may assume, therefore, that Jonah went to Nineveh this time because he was afraid to run away again. He went, though, and gave God's message in the briefest possible form; Jonah's actual prophetic oracle to Nineveh is just five words in the Hebrew.

Pagan Nineveh repented! For the second time, Jonah had resisted giving any but the barest word of grace. For the second time, in spite of Jonah—not because of him—pagans responded. For the second time, God delivered a group of pagan non-Israelites.

God . . . had compassion (3:10); this verb often is translated "relented." For God to withhold or delay a threatened judgment is both to relent and to have compassion. God's relenting of judgment always is a demonstration of His compassion, especially in the face of genuine repentance like the people of Nineveh demonstrated.

God Confronted Jonah (Jon. 4:9–11)

Jonah did not share God's compassion toward Nineveh. When God answered his complaint with a question, Jonah did not deign to answer, but went outside the city and sulked. He tied a square of cloth to four poles for shade over his head. A fast-growing plant (perhaps a **vine** [v. 10]) added shade and moisture; by the next day a worm had killed the plant. For a second time, Jonah asked to die. For a second time, God asked Jonah, **"Do you have a right to be angry?"** (v. 9). This time, Jonah was provoked enough to answer, **"I do"** (v. 9).

God's final response to Jonah ends the book on a rhetorical question that the reader, no less than Jonah, is to carry away from this series of events. God set up a contrast between the plant and the city. Jonah took care for a single plant (**vine**), which he had not caused to become great (**make it grow** [v. 10]). Did not God have the right to take care (same Hebrew verb) of Nineveh, the great city (same Hebrew root) of more than 120,000 persons, and many animals?

WORDS FROM WESLEY
Jonah 4:11

I—The God of infinite compassions and goodness. *That great city*—Wouldest thou have me less merciful to such a goodly city, than thou art to a weed? *Who cannot discern*—Here are more than six-score innocents who are infants. *Much cattle*—Beside men, women and children who are in Nineveh, there are many other of my creatures that are not sinful, and my tender mercies are and shall be over all my works. If thou wouldest be their butcher, yet I will be their God. Go Jonah, rest thyself content and be thankful: that goodness, which spared Nineveh, hath spared thee in this thy inexcusable frowardness. I will be to repenting Nineveh what I am to thee, a God gracious and merciful, slow to anger, and of great kindness, and I will turn from the evil which thou and they deserve. (ENOT)

Who cannot tell their right hand from their left (v. 11) sometimes is taken to mean "children." Rather, it is a way of saying Nineveh's people did not have the moral discernment between right and wrong in which God had instructed Israel. The vivid lesson of God's final rhetorical question to Jonah echoes through the centuries when we read this book. What "enemies" do we wish God would take care of for us? What is God's attitude toward them?

DISCUSSION

Discuss how you can know when God is speaking to you. Share a time when this happened to you.

1. Jonah was angry with the Ninevites and didn't want them to be saved. What people of the world, if any, are you angry with? Do you want them to be saved? Why or why not?

2. How would you respond if God commanded you to preach salvation to your worst enemy? Do you think Jonah's response is understandable? Acceptable?

3. Jonah chose to physically flee from God's will. By what other actions do people sometimes avoid doing the will of God?

4. God was aggressive in gaining Jonah's compliance with His will. Has God ever done something unexpected to gain your attention or obedience?

5. How would you rate your enthusiasm about accomplishing God's mission among people who are outside your country or cultural group?

6. Unexpected spiritual benefits resulted from the storm Jonah experienced. Have you seen examples of spiritual gain from hardship in your own life? How so?

7. It took three days and nights for Jonah to admit that the great fish was God's answer to his call for help. Is there something in your life that could be an unrecognized answer to prayer?

8. What characteristic of God do you see most prominently illustrated by the story of Jonah?

9. In what ways might you be like Jonah?

PRAYER

Father, You have asked us to go and tell others that You love them and want to save them from their sins. Forgive us for the times we have not done that. We want to be willing servants. Help us to love others in the same way You love them.

6

WHAT GOD REQUIRES

Micah 3:1–7; 6:1–8

If we love God, we will respond to the needs of others.

The abuse of power is a particularly despicable sin. While we may easily pardon a substance abuser for what we see as a "weakness," we are generally tough on CEOs who raid retiree pension funds, nonprofit executives who divert donations for their private use, or politicians who steal from the public till. We abhor those who use their power to take advantage of the helpless or needy. God does too.

Through the prophet Micah, God condemns leaders who abuse their power, and He extends that condemnation to all who have forsaken their trust. It isn't just CEOs and power brokers who may advance themselves at the expense of the needy. Any of us may be guilty of enriching ourselves while ignoring the plight of those around us.

Just as God extends His grace to us when we are helpless in sin, He expects us to spread His love to all who are in need. This is a central message in Scripture, but one that is often ignored. Sometimes, after we personally receive God's grace, we forget to pass it on. This study calls us back to the vital truth that the blessings we receive from God are meant to be shared with others.

COMMENTARY

Micah dealt with social injustice on a large scale. The book of Micah can be divided into three sections: chapters 1–2, 3–4, and 5–7. Each division includes a call to listen, a statement of

the problem, a pronouncement of coming judgment, and a promise of hope.

Call to Listen (Mic. 3:1–7)

In chapter 3, Micah confronted the wayward leaders of Israel.
He began with a call to listen to the voice of the Lord: **"Listen,
you leaders of Jacob"** (v. 1). He used similar phrases at the
beginning of the other two sections as well (see 1:2; 6:1). God
is pleased when we listen to Him. It is hard on us when we act
like stubborn mules that have to be led with a bridle. As the
psalmist wrote, "Do not be like the horse or the mule, which have
no understanding but must be controlled by bit and bridle or they
will not come to you" (Ps. 32:9). Jesus stated it like this: "He
who has ears, let him hear" (Matt. 11:15; see also 13:9, 43; Mark
4:23; Luke 14:35; Rev. 2:7). It is to our personal advantage to
listen to the voice of the Lord. Additionally, our nation benefits
when we listen and are obedient to the will of God for our lives.
"Righteousness exalts a nation," says the writer of Proverbs
(14:34).

Problems. Micah called the leaders of Israel to accept their
responsibility for justice: **"Should you not know justice"**
(Mic. 3:1). He berated them for hating good and loving evil.
His accusation depicted shepherds who were not only not good
shepherds, but they intentionally harmed and mutilated their
sheep. The description Micah used is probably symbolic and
includes skinning, deboning, chopping up, cooking, and eating
the flesh of their sheep. The contrast with Jesus is stark and vivid.
Jesus is the Good Shepherd who laid down His life for the sheep.
These rulers of Israel oppressed the poor and denied them the
justice they so desperately needed.

WORDS FROM WESLEY

Micah 3:2

The good—Ye who hate not only to do good, but the good which is done, and those that do it. *The evil*—Chuse, and delight in both evil works and evil workers. *Who pluck off*—Ye who use the flock as cruelly as the shepherd, who instead of sheering the fleece, would pluck off the skin and flesh. (ENOT)

Israel's leaders were corrupt and Micah confronted them. In verse 4, Micah told them the Lord would not hear their cry if they did not hear the cries of their people. He also stated that God **will hide his face from them**. It is a scary thought that God would hide His face. He is the sovereign Creator of the universe. Everything exists and is sustained by the touch of His hand, the whisper of His voice, the grace of His Spirit. To think that the very One who is in complete control of the universe would turn His face is a sobering thought. It makes one wonder what the world would be like without the restraining influence of godliness.

It would be bad enough if corruption ended with the political leaders of Israel, but it had infiltrated the people's faith and worship as well. In verse 5, Micah confronted the prophets, who were scandals in their own right, accusing them of leading God's **people astray**.

It appears the corrupt clergy of Micah's day would prophesy times of peacefulness if their parishioners would **feed** (v. 5) them. Today's equivalency would be this: "For enough money you can hear whatever sermon you want to hear." They gave themselves to saying what the itching ears of the people wanted to hear. None of this escaped the watchful eye of the Lord and His good prophet Micah.

Judgment. Micah described God's judgment on wayward prophets as nights **without visions, and darkness, without**

divination (v. 6), and dark days without the sun. He meant they would endure seasons of spiritual darkness when they could not hear from God. The implication of this is also that God would not come to their aid when they needed Him. They would be castaways from the kingdom because of their sinful leadership.

WORDS FROM WESLEY

Micah 3:7

The seers—So called by the deceived people. *Cover their lips*—Mourners did thus, Ezek. 24:17, 22. So these shall mourn and pine in their shame. *No answer*—Because the answer they had formerly, pretended to be from God, now appears not to have been from Him. (ENOT)

Court in Session and Divine Dialogue (Mic. 6:1–8)

This section has the feel of a courtroom. It is as if God is putting Israel on trial and they are called to give an accounting for their deeds: **Stand up, plead your case. . . . Hear . . . the LORD's accusation** (vv. 1–2). He was lodging a charge against Israel. Who can stand in the great and awful day of divine interrogation? Israel could not stand on its own merits. It was overflowing with injustice and oppression of the poor.

WORDS FROM WESLEY

Micah 6:1

Arise—This is God's command to Micah. *Contend thou*—Argue the case between God and thy people; and speak as if thou wouldst make the mountains hear thee, to testify for me. (ENOT)

We are all sinners. Our only hope is redemption by the forgiving grace of God through the atoning sacrifice of His only begotten Son, our Lord and Savior, Jesus Christ. With that in mind, the corrupt officials and priests of Israel did not stand a chance. They may have thought their actions were escaping the notice of the Creator, but just as He saw the plight of His children during their slavery in Egypt, so He also noticed their oppressive leaders during the days of Micah. The distinguished Judge of all the earth has taken His seat, and Israel's day in court has begun.

Verse 3 appears to be a rhetorical question. God already knew the answer but asked anyway, **"What have I done to you? How have I burdened you?"** This is one of those times when Israel stood speechless before God. Like Adam and Eve, Israel sinned and could not cover it up. All things are laid bare and open before Him who is omniscient.

Balak king of Moab tried to bribe **Balaam** (v. 5) into prophesying a curse on the nation of Israel. Balaam was warned by God not to do so, and he refused the repeated attempts of the king to curse Israel. This story from Israel's past reflects the conditions of their present.

The **journey from Shittim to Gigal** (v. 5) reminds us of God's miracles in bringing Israel out of Egypt. He parted the Red Sea and the Jordan River. Shittim was Israel's last campsite before crossing the Jordan River to take possession of the Promised Land (Josh. 3:1). It was also the town from which Joshua sent the spies to explore the land (Josh. 2:1). Gilgal was their first campsite after crossing the Jordan River (Josh. 3:1). It was there that they erected the twelve stones as a memorial for God's miraculous intervention (Josh. 4:19–20). Shittim to Gilgal was from one side of the Jordan River to the other side. This represented God's blessing of giving them the land. God was reminding them of what He had done for them, which was not burdensome.

Note that the name used by Micah for God is "LORD." It is small capitals in the English translation, which means it is the

Hebrew term *YHWH*. YHWH is the name God gave for himself to Moses. Because it has no vowels, scholars still debate its pronunciation. The important truth to know about this name for God is that it is specifically associated with the Hebrew God. When that name was used, listeners or readers knew exactly which deity was being referenced. When the name YHWH or LORD is used, there is no doubt about whom the prophet was speaking.

The final three verses of this passage speak about Israel's coming before the Lord with some kind of offering or sacrifice. **Burnt offerings** and **calves a year old** (Mic. 6:6) were typical sacrifices for that day. Would the Almighty be pleased with such offerings from corrupt leaders and wayward clergy? What if there were **thousands of rams** and **rivers of oil** (v. 7)? Would a multitude of sacrifices be better than a few? What if they even went so far as to offer their **firstborn** for the sin of their souls? Would the Lord be more pleased with human sacrifice than the offering of animals and oil? The answer to all of these scenarios is no.

There are times when it is appropriate to give large offerings to the Lord. Solomon offered thousands of animals as sacrifices when celebrating the dedication of the temple (1 Kings 8:63). In the New Testament, a woman poured an alabaster jar of very expensive perfume on Jesus' head (Matt. 26:7). It was a sacrifice of great financial proportions, so there are times when extravagant giving is acceptable and appropriate. However, it is an abomination to God to give sacrificial or very expensive offerings to Him or His church with the thought that the gift itself would somehow gain His favor and cause Him to forgive our sins. Although the Israelites could bribe their clergy and perhaps their politicians too, they could not bribe God.

Micah 6:8 answers the rhetorical questions and problems of public and church leadership. It is a verse worthy of memorization and implementation: **He has showed you, O man, what is good.**

And what does the LORD require of you? To act justly and to love mercy and to walk humbly with your God.

The requirements of the Lord are those aspects of our spiritual life for which He is searching. These are the qualities He is looking for in His kingdom people: to act justly; to love mercy, and to walk humbly with Him.

WORDS FROM WESLEY

Micah 6:8

He—God hath already told you in His Word, with what you ought to come before Him. *To do justly*—To render to every one their due, superiors, equals, inferiors, to be equal to all, and oppress none, in body, goods or name; in all your dealings with men carry a chancery in your own beasts, and do according to equity. *To love mercy*—To be kind, merciful and compassionate to all not using severity towards any. *Walk humbly with thy God*—Keep up a constant fellowship with God, by humble, holy faith. (ENOT)

To act justly is the opposite of what the corrupt leaders in Israel were doing. They were oppressing the people and leading them astray. God is looking for people who are honest, unbiased, moral, truthful, faithful, and who refuse to take bribes. There are many honest people in the world, but only those who are committed to serving the Lord can be totally honest from the inside out.

To walk humbly with God is a requirement and privilege for us all. It is humbling to think that the Lord of all the earth, the sovereign Creator of the universe, is willing to let us walk with Him. He is so much greater. His thoughts are higher. His ways are mysterious. We are fortunate, indeed, to walk with our God, and such a privilege is humbling.

The cure for the corruption that plagued Israel and plagues the church was and is found in justice, lovingkindness, and humble spirituality. These three make a powerful trilogy that is just as effective and influential today as it was for Micah's generation. When we give ourselves to doing these three deeds, we are changed for the better. Our transformation, in turn, transforms our communities. Our transformed communities transform our nation and our world. And yet, it all begins with a personal relationship with our God. Walk humbly with Him.

DISCUSSION

Share about a time you were called for jury duty. Discuss why you enjoyed it or not.

1. What makes a just or righteous leader? Name some examples of just and unjust leaders, either historical or present-day.

2. Micah pointed out that some people who disobey God still cry out to Him and expect help. Why do you think people do that? Have you seen examples of this in your culture? Have you ever done this?

3. Even spiritual leaders can sometimes be bought with a price or a favor. What do you think causes a spiritual leader to abandon his or her responsibility?

4. In the court case that God brings against Israel in this Scripture, what evidence is entered? If God were to bring your nation into court, what charges could be leveled? What evidence would be brought?

5. The Israelites have not been the only people to complain against God and feel that His commands are burdensome. Can you name others? In what ways might your church—or you personally—have done this?

6. Why do you think it is so easy for people to forget what God has done in the past?

7. In what ways do people try to appease God when they sense He is angry? Which ways are not effective? What is effective?

PRAYER

Father, there is so much noise in our world and so many influences that would try to shape the direction of our lives. We need the direction and correction that comes from hearing from You. May we have the spirit of Samuel so we will say, "Speak, Lord, for your servant is listening."

7

GOD REIGNS AND RESTORES

Nahum 1:1—2:2

The Lord protects and rewards those who trust Him.

For a parent, which is more important: discipline or affirmation? Which is the most important ingredient in a marriage: accountability or trust? Which is most helpful to a coach in training athletes: reward or punishment? Obviously, both are needed in each case. Typically, however, we emphasize one or the other. A parent may be either too permissive or too demanding. A spouse may fall into the error of being too trusting or too controlling. We often cast God in that same light, emphasizing either His strict justice or His loving mercy. Many people, believing that God is only demanding, harsh, and judgmental, feel alienated from Him.

Spending time exploring the Minor Prophets, one might conclude that God is a God of pure justice. Judgment seems written on every page. Yet this study delivers a message of good news about God's great love. We have already seen that God showed His love by giving Nineveh a chance to repent. Now God brings His love to its fulfillment in Judah.

This study will bring good news to those who have felt from God only a message of condemnation. God's grace is as real and as powerful as His justice, and there will come a day when He restores all things.

COMMENTARY

The book of Nahum was written years after the spiritual revival that Jonah's preaching brought about in Nineveh. In Nahum we read the same message, but this time Nineveh paid no attention. The revival that turned back God's wrath against Assyria had long since cooled. In this book, Assyria is an impressive, powerful nation characterized by her destruction and her cruelty among the nations. Although she was once God's instrument of chastisement, she has become an enemy of God. Her arrogance is evident in all she does. Her magnificent and crushing rule extends from the Nile to the Tigris.

It is commonly accepted that the writing of Nahum took place during the reign of Hezekiah, when Judah felt the yoke of oppression by Assyria (1:13).

God is the principal character in Nahum. We see that He is in complete and total authority over the nations and creation. The book is clearly a message to His people, Judah, even though they are mentioned only a few times. This message says Assyria's hold over Judah is entirely in the hands of God. Judah must turn to Him if there is to be any future for the people.

In the book of Nahum, the Assyrians become the medium that God used to display His power and justice. We must not miss the import of this book that says we are all open to God's judgment. Judah knew this. They were feeling the effects of God's discipline. There were Nineveh-like tendencies in them that brought them to this place of utter devastation. Do we have the same pride, arrogance, and self-reliance working its way into our hearts? The book of Nahum is here to give us all warning, and we must listen. God is jealous for our affection and trust. He desires a continual trust and reliance born out of an ongoing relationship.

The Contents of the Book (Nah. 1:1)

Who was Nahum? We know two things about his life: his name and his hometown. That is all. Nahum's name means "consolation" or "full of comfort." It is through this prophet we know that God had not forgotten Judah. With His judgment, He offers restoration, but the key is our response to His discipline. Do we continue in our sin as Nineveh did, or do we turn back to God as Judah did?

Nahum opens with a title telling us what will play out in the following chapters. The fact that we read **an oracle concerning Nineveh** (v. 1) before we read that this is a book by Nahum suggests its negative and ominous content. The word *oracle* means burden. The verb form has the meaning of the duty of carrying the sacred vessels of the temple or tabernacle. This message that Nahum brought was a burden of the most sacred kind. It was God revealing His heart to His people and Nineveh. It is also connected with judgment and the burden that it brings. It is a word that weighed heavy on the heart of the prophet and on the heart of God.

The book of the vision of Nahum the Elkoshite (v. 1). Nahum had a vision. This was not a dream but a revelation from God. Nahum spoke without any hesitation, even though his message meant bad news for the world's superpower at the time.

God's Character Revealed (Nah. 1:2–7)

The prophetic revelation opened with force that does not let up for the next three chapters. **The LORD is a jealous and avenging God** (v. 2). This form of the word *jealous* is used only twice and outside of the Pentateuch. It is used solely of God in the context of idolatry. Idolatry is spiritual adultery and merits death, just as God's law states for adultery of any kind. God tolerates no rivals. Here in verse 2, the name of God used is His personal name, Yahweh (**LORD**), a name that connotes a closeness of relationship.

WORDS FROM WESLEY

Nahum 1:2

Revengeth—As supreme governor, who by office is bound to right the oppressed, and to punish the oppressor. (ENOT)

What was Yahweh jealous about? God was jealous for His people. God was Judah's husband, and they prostituted themselves and went after other gods. God wanted their exclusive affection because their affection in any other place would ultimately debase themselves. This crisis came upon them because of their wandering hearts. The real destruction of God's people began the moment they turned their affections away to other loves. In God's faithfulness, He was trying to reclaim them through His loving discipline. If He did not care about them, He would have abandoned them long ago (Heb. 12:10).

Coupled with God's jealousy is His vengeance, a quality only fit for the hands of God. He alone has the justice, the purity, and the scope to mete it out. We can be encouraged that God is aware of all unrestrained injustice, and in the end He will vindicate all His children who have been wronged.

Although God maintains His wrath against His enemies, **the LORD is slow to anger and great in power** (v. 3). This does not weaken His wrath, but gives time for the foes of God to turn from their ways. This "slowness" is a good thing because He **will not leave the guilty unpunished** (v. 3). That includes all of us. His measuring stick does not change for anyone.

In Nahum 1:4–6, we read of God's power as He controls all of creation. No person or thing can escape His presence or dominion. **Who can withstand his indignation? Who can endure his fierce anger** (v. 6)? These rhetorical questions demand the admission that no one can. But because God is jealous for us, He seeks and desires us. We know this from the following verse.

The LORD is good (v. 7). We can trust in His complete and unspotted goodness. God is entirely saturated in beautiful righteousness. All He does is grounded in His benevolence. He is **a refuge in times of trouble. He cares for those who trust in him** (v. 7). God offers a place of shelter and safekeeping, but we must trust Him.

Nineveh's Character Exposed (Nah. 1:8–11)

But with an overwhelming flood he will make an end of Nineveh (v. 8). Evidence shows that Nineveh was totally destroyed by both flood and fire. It was never rebuilt. This was pretty unusual in history; typically famous cities remained, while rulers came and went. Not in this case. Not a stone of the city was uncovered until the mid 1800s when an archeologist went looking for this lost city.

WORDS FROM WESLEY

Nahum 1:8

An over-running flood—His judgments like a mighty flood that overflows all banks, shall swallow up Assyria. *Thereof*—Of Nineveh, that is, Nineveh itself. *Darkness*—Troubles and desolating afflictions. (ENOT)

Why was God so angry with this empire? **From you, O Nineveh, has one come forth who plots evil against the LORD and counsels wickedness** (v. 11). Nineveh was an enemy of the most blasphemous kind. Chapter 3 calls her a "city of blood, full of lies" and "never without victims" (3:1). The "piles of dead" (3:3) are abundant, "all because of the wanton lust of a harlot" (3:4). The worship of pagan gods was Ninevah's specialty, called the "mistress of sorceries," enslaving nations by witchcraft (3:4). Ninevah's dominance was both physical and spiritual.

Judah's Restoration Assured (Nah. 1:12—2:2)

The tone of the book shifts as the Lord talked directly and lovingly to Judah. **"Although I have afflicted you, O Judah, I will afflict you no more"** (1:12). We see clearly that Nineveh was never really Judah's major concern. It was God who afflicted Judah to prompt repentance. It was in His design to bring Judah's heart back to where it belonged. God's wrath turned because Judah had finally turned back to Him. That was Judah's only hope.

Look, there on the mountains, the feet of one who brings good news (1:15). Deliverance was so sure that the arrival of a messenger who brought the announcement of the enemy's defeat could already be seen. When God says something, it is as good as done. Salvation comes both materially and spiritually.

WORDS FROM WESLEY

Nahum 1:15

Sinners, with joy look up!
The herald's feet appear,
He comes from Zion's sacred top,
A gospel-messenger!
Good news he publishes
Of all mankind forgiven,
Salvation sent from God, and peace
Restored 'twixt earth and heaven.
Peace from above reveal'd,
Which never shall depart,
Peace by the Spirits signet seal'd
On every faithful heart;
The end of war and sin
In Christ your peace obtain:
And when His kingdom reigns within,
It shall for ever reign. (PW, vol. 10, 100–101)

No more will the wicked invade you; they will be completely destroyed (1:15). The victory is sure and it will be complete. This enemy of Judah won't be back. God promised the complete destruction of Nineveh. Complete freedom from the wicked, however, was conditional on Judah's obedience. And, as we see later, they chose to disobey and were exiled as a result.

The Lord will restore the splendor of Jacob (2:2). God's desire is to bring about restoration, reestablishing a relationship with His people to himself. It is interesting and fundamental to realize where the restoration would begin for Judah: in their emptiness.

God's people will be restored **though destroyers have laid them waste and have ruined their vines** (2:2). Judah was entirely without ability to begin again. God promised to restore Judah physically and spiritually from a place of extreme barrenness. No longer would Judah rely on its vines but on the True Vine. God as the gardener pruned the branches so that they would bear *more* fruit. God can bring even greater fruitfulness and splendor to our lives after we have received and accepted His discipline.

WORDS FROM WESLEY

Nahum 2:2

For—Israel and Jacob were more to God, yet He punished them; much more will He punish Nineveh. *Turned*—Laid low. *The excellency*—The wealth, the valiant men, all that Jacob gloried in. *Jacob*—The two tribes. *Israel*—The ten tribes. *Emptied them*—Quite exhausted them. *Their vine branches*—Destroyed all the fruit of the land. (ENOT)

DISCUSSION

Share a time when you were afraid of God.

1. What is your reaction to the description of God in Nahum 1:1–2?

2. What might cause God to be jealous, full of wrath, and seeking vengeance?

3. What is your reaction to the description of God in 1:3?

4. Nahum's doomsday message was given to Nineveh about 150 years after Jonah's message of mercy. What lessons can you draw from that fact about God's character?

5. Nineveh was a powerful warrior state, wealthy from the looting of other nations. How might they have reacted to Nahum's description of God's power in 1:3–6? What is your reaction?

6. What nations on earth today could be compared to Nineveh?

7. How do you reconcile the description of God in 1:7 with the way He is described in 1:3–6?

8. Why do you think people found it so difficult to trust God back then? Are those the same reasons that people find it hard to trust Him now? Are there other reasons today?

9. Does the prediction about the fall of Nineveh bring you comfort or anxiety?

PRAYER

Father, we don't always understand it when You are good to those who do us harm. At times Your purposes are beyond our understanding. But we have learned to trust You, and we find refuge in Your loving care for us.

8

REVIVE US AGAIN!

Habakkuk 1:11; 3:2, 17–19

We need ongoing spiritual renewal to maintain
our relationship with God.

Can you imagine what it would be like if the spiritual life was as visible as the physical? Undoubtedly we would see some sad-looking, wilted people! What would a spiritual assessment reveal about your inner life? Would it show that you are 25 percent dry or 90 percent lifeless? If so, revival is needed.

This study gives us a recipe for spiritual renewal in the form of a dialogue between Habakkuk and God. Although the prophet comes with questions, he demonstrated the attitude of reverence and trust that will always lead to a renewed relationship with God. As you follow this frank and honest exchange, you will be led to open your own heart to God and be revived.

COMMENTARY

Have you ever pondered the question why? When we consider our lives and the world around us, we often wonder why things are the way they are and when they will be changed. Whenever the "why" question is asked, it's usually in the context of despondency: Why is there so much evil around me? Why did God allow such a good person to die? Why are seemingly evil people rewarded, while people of integrity struggle?

Consider the fact that even Jesus asked why as He hung on the cross. He had surrendered to His Father's will, lived a sinless life, yet He was seemingly forsaken by His loving heavenly Father as He died for others.

Today the question of why has never been more relevant. Never have the words of the prophet Isaiah been so alarmingly fitting: "Woe to those who call evil good and good evil, who put darkness for light and light for darkness, who put bitter for sweet and sweet for bitter" (5:20). The prophet spoke of a world where good is bad and bad is good. For anyone who has ever looked around this world and asked why, the prophet Habakkuk is indeed a spokesperson, and the answer he received will lift the heaviest of hearts.

The book of Habakkuk contains a dialogue between the prophet and God. In the first two chapters, Habakkuk argued with God over His ways that appeared unfathomable, if not unjust to the prophet. God responded, and Habakkuk made a beautiful confession of faith in the last chapter.

This account of wrestling with God is composed for Israel. No doubt it represented the voice of the godly in Judah struggling to comprehend God's ways. God's answers spoke to anyone who shared Habakkuk's troubled thoughts. Habakkuk's faith confession became a public expression as a liturgy.

Why Such Injustice? (Hab. 1:11)

As much as he was a prophet, Habakkuk was also a poet. The insight he possessed along with the quality with which he wrote point as much to the sensitive poet as they do to the thundering prophet.

He wrote his book about 605 BC. Habakkuk, whose name means "to embrace," is believed to have been a musician of the Levitical office who took part in temple worship singing. He was a contemporary of Jeremiah. Habakkuk was a prophet who embraced the times in which he lived. What he saw troubled him. Living during the reign of evil King Jehoiakim (609–598 BC), the prophet was well aware of the world's new power, Babylon. This menacing empire had its sights set on Jerusalem. It did not help Habakkuk that God told him in verses 5–10 that Babylon would indeed conquer Jerusalem and that the prophet would live to see it. This prophecy is generally dated a little before or after the battle of Carchemish (605 BC), when Egyptian forces, who had earlier gone to the aid of the last Assyrian king, were routed by the Babylonians under Nabopolassar and Nebuchadnezzar and were pursued as far as the Egyptian border (Jer. 46). That Habakkuk's hopes were brought to despair would only heighten his joy when the Lord would disclose to him His full revelation.

Though King Jehoiakim's father, King Josiah, had been a great king with godly convictions, Jehoiakim had no interest in emulating his father's righteousness. He reigned for eleven years. At the beginning of his reign, Judah was subject to Egypt. Probably in 605 BC, however, Babylon defeated Egypt. Jehoiakim, who apparently had been content to be a vassal of Egypt, transferred his allegiance to Babylon.

Habakkuk began his short book by asking four questions in verses 2 and 3:

1. "How long, O LORD, must I call for help, but you do not listen?"
2. "Or cry out to you, 'Violence!' but you do not save?"
3. "Why do you make me look at injustice?"
4. "Why do you tolerate wrong?"

He then followed with a cause-and-effect observation. Destruction and violence were manifest in society. Strife and conflict abounded everywhere. It seemed the wicked were the ones profiting the most, while the righteous were trampled underfoot. Those who struggle to follow God's ways are often branded as extremists and intolerant. Just as Habakkuk cried to God for an answer, so today do we who seek justice cry out, "Why?"

God's answer to the prophet was basically, "You think things are bad now? They will get even worse." The whole purpose of the Babylonian captivity of the southern kingdom of Judah was judgment for its many years of sin (Jer. 25:7–11). **Then they sweep past like the wind and go on** (Hab. 1:11) illustrates the swiftness and terror with which the Babylonians would strike. They were **guilty men, whose own strength** was **their god** (v. 11). The Babylonians were so proud and confident of their military might that it had virtually become an object of worship.

WORDS FROM WESLEY

Habakkuk 1:11

Bitter—Cruel, and without mercy. *Hasty*—Speedy in executing their merciless purposes. (ENOT, Hab. 1:6)

Why Fear Any Longer? (Hab. 3:2)

For Habakkuk, this entire experience had been an emotional roller coaster. He began at the brink of despair, but now was at the height of exaltation after Jehovah's response in chapter 2. He had been given a glimpse of God's sovereignty. God is the supreme Judge and sole executioner of His judgment. Habakkuk's eyes moved from the problems of his day to the One who would one day bring all wickedness to an end. We should take such a view. We are not a defeated people. God is our Victor, and He will allow nothing to happen apart from His perfect will.

The poet prophet wrote, **LORD, I have heard of your fame** (v. 2) as a celebration of God's mighty saving acts of old. **I stand in awe of your deeds, O LORD** (v. 2) indicates the reverence Habakkuk had for the historical evidence of God's mighty hand at work. In fact, he provided a brief list of the attributes of God from verses 3–14. Can we not all testify to the Almighty's intervention on our behalf at some time in our lives?

Renew them in our day (v. 2), cried the prophet. He pleaded for a revival among his people. With the threat of imminent invasion, he pleaded with the Sovereign, **in our time make them known** (v. 2). His request was that somehow God would reveal himself to His people once again through a spiritual awakening. Despite the coming destruction, **in wrath remember mercy** (v. 2).

WORDS FROM WESLEY

Habakkuk 3:2

Father of everlasting grace,
Revive Thy work of righteousness,
Even in these dregs of time make known
Thy truth and mercy in Thy Son;
O call His precious death to mind,
That ransom paid for all mankind,
Thine anger with our sins remove,
And show the world Thy pardoning love. (PW, vol. 10, 103)

Why Not Rejoice? (Hab. 3:17–19)

What began in despair ended in elation. Knowing that God was in complete control of all the world's activities, the prophet determined that he would not let the worries of the world dismay him any longer. Habakkuk decided to change his attitude and approach to life.

Though the fig tree does not bud and there are no grapes on the vines, though the olive crop fails and the fields produce no food, though there are no sheep in the pen and no cattle in the stalls (v. 17) is an anticipation of the results of the Babylonian invasion and devastation. This was an agricultural society, so the currency is explained in terms of crops and livestock. The olive crop was the basis for olive oil, a fundamental liquid for ancient Israel. Olive oil was essential to the diet, used for medicinal purposes, and valued as a fuel for lamps.

WORDS FROM WESLEY

Habakkuk 3:17

When I heard—What dreadful desolations God threatened against Israel. *My heart trembled*—Another effect of surprising fears and astonishment. *Rottenness*—A decay of all my strength. *That I might rest*—These fears made me betake myself to God, that I might rest in Him. *He*—The king of Babylon. *The people*—The *Jews*. (ENOT, Hab. 3:16)

One of the great uplifting passages in all of Scripture shows that Habakkuk in his exaltation was still a realist. We might have trouble meeting all of our expenses. Maybe the cupboards can get a little bare. The paycheck may not seem to stretch like it once did. Perhaps things are falling apart in our personal lives. It may not be through any fault of our own, since, like Habakkuk, we are trying to live godly lives. This study reminds us that at times God does allow difficulties to interrupt our lives. Problems may continue despite the depth of our faith, but Habakkuk determined, **yet I will rejoice in the LORD** (v. 18). He made a conscious decision: Despite circumstances, **I will be joyful in God my Savior** (v. 18). Every one of us makes a daily choice about our attitude. Despite the things that may be happening in the world around us, we can take joy in the Lord of our salvation. He alone is our strength and the only One capable of lifting our spirits when things appear gloomy.

Habakkuk learned the lesson of faith because, he said, **The Sovereign LORD is my strength** (v. 19). He trusted in God's providence regardless of circumstances. He declared that even if God should send suffering and loss, he would still rejoice in his Savior-God—one of the strongest affirmations of faith in all of Scripture. Imagine knowing that at any moment, life as you know it could come to a swift end. God just showed Habakkuk the certainty of

Babylonian invasion, yet Habakkuk was able to sing, God **makes my feet like the feet of a deer** (v. 19). If you have ever observed these creatures, you know they are nimble and sure-footed. They are able to leap tall obstacles with slight effort. With this thought in mind, Habakkuk reminded his readers that it is God who will enable His people to overcome. God has no desire for us to wallow in despair, but instead **he enables** us **to go on the heights** (v. 19). Satan would love for Christians to be despondent and succumb to trying situations. Yet, God has given us the ability to experience revival in our hearts each day as we meditate on His Word and make a determined effort to focus our thoughts on our all-powerful and loving Lord.

The book of Habakkuk encourages us not to despair over the evils of this world and not to let our lives be controlled by what we see. We are inspired by Habakkuk's words to wait patiently on the Lord.

WORDS FROM WESLEY
Habakkuk 3:19

Like hinds feet—That I may escape to God my refuge. *He will make me*—To conquer and triumph. (ENOT)

DISCUSSION

Discuss whether or not you think people are honest with God.

1. Habakkuk was being honest when he complained about the injustices of the world. What injustices bother you so much that you would to complain to God about them?

2. Habakkuk 1:11 describes invading armies who brought devastation and then moved on. How do you react when violent people (or nations) seem to advance in impunity?

3. Habakkuk described people as having "strength" as their god. What gods do people rely on today?

4. If someone overheard you talking about God, what image of Him do you think would come to their minds?

5. In what ways does your church remember and rehearse the famous, awesome deeds of God? What do you risk when you fail to do this?

6. Do you remember times when God's activity was more evident in your life or church than today? What was different then that caused it to be so special?

7. What does the phrase "in wrath remember mercy" tell us about Habakkuk's understanding of God? How might that prayer be needed in today?

8. If you were to list the hardships in your life, how would it compare with the list in 3:17?

9. How do people typically cope with hard times? How do you? Based on this study, what advice would you give to those who are facing trauma?

PRAYER

Father, we live in a world that suffers from the consequences of sin. Though we are not always protected from these consequences, You are always near us in our times of difficulty, giving us strength, courage, and hope. What we know about You causes us to trust when we don't know what lies ahead.

9

GOD IS FAITHFUL

Zephaniah 3:7–20

God always keeps His word.

Every person must determine the answer to two questions about God. The first is whether God exists. The second concerns the character of God. Is God good? This question gets at what theologians have called the problem of evil. Faced with the fact that bad things happen to good people, many conclude that God, while ever present, is essentially powerless to do anything about evil in the world—or simply doesn't want to.

Neither is true. God is both good and just, both Comforter and Judge. In time, He will deliver His people from whatever threatens to harm them. We see this illustrated in the book of Zephaniah and take confidence that evil will never ultimately triumph and God will never abandon His people to final defeat. This study offers consolation and hope to those who are tempted to doubt God. It affirms that God is both good and powerful, both loving and just. His judgment is accompanied by an incredible promise of hope. In the worst of times, God still has His people at heart and refuses to desert them.

COMMENTARY

Zephaniah prophesied during the reign of King Josiah, 639–609 BC, but probably before the reformation of 621. Unlike Micah, who was concerned with the common person, Zephaniah positioned his prophecy in royal context. He made a point of his own family link to the great King Hezekiah, who was king of

Judah 715–687 BC. His prophecy shows knowledge of the court; thus Zephaniah was more of a prophet to the princes than to the people. This makes sense because Josiah came to the throne as a boy and was guided by prophets and other mentors until his maturity.

Assyria was the enemy that would bring about the day of the Lord. Thus the theological context is eschatological—when God will finally and completely destroy His enemies and all evil.

The passage studied here is one of redemption and hope. This fits well with the eschatological tenor of the entire prophecy. Unfortunately, because of the extreme misuse of Revelation, eschatology is viewed with suspicion and fear. The biblical reality is far different. The "end" means the end of evil and the restoration of good to its rightful place within the commonwealth of creation.

Fear and Redemption (Zeph. 3:7–10)

It may seem odd that a prophecy given to a people so racked with fear should contain yet more fear. However, the fact is that we live in a frightful and dangerous world. Jesus said, "In this world you will have trouble" (John 16:33). The question, then, is twofold: How do we handle the fear, and what or whom do we fear the most?

Zephaniah 3:7 answers question 2 succinctly: **Surely you will fear me** [God] **and accept correction!** It is as old as creation itself: "The fear of the Lord—that is wisdom, and to shun evil is understanding" (Job 28:28). It appears that we may have more to fear than simply fear itself. We can either choose to live in denial (as if we can control our world and, thus, remove anything fearful), or we can turn to God, fear Him, receive correction, and be purified.

It is interesting that purification begins with the lips (Zeph. 3:9). This fits well with the call of Isaiah (ch. 6), James' admonition to control the tongue (1:26; 3:1–12), and Jesus' claim that uncleanness comes out of the mouth from the overflow of the heart (Matt. 12:34). It also leads well into the result—**that all of them may call on the name of the LORD** (Zeph. 3:9), which is a key to both God's grace and His salvation in the Old Testament (see Joel 2:32). This theme is so important that Paul actually quoted this verse in Romans 10:13.

So how do we answer the first question? **"Therefore wait for me," declares the LORD, "for the day I will stand to testify"** (Zeph. 3:8). Faith in God demands patience. It also demands belief in the day of the Lord, when God himself will right the wrong. Too often, we get ahead of God and try to accomplish His ends in our own power.

WORDS FROM WESLEY

Zephaniah 3:8

Therefore—Since you will not be amended. *Wait ye*—Attend my resolution. *Until*—Until I rise up to destroy first, and next to take the spoil. *Upon them*—The incorrigible Jews. *Devoured*—Consumed as if burnt up. *My jealousy*—That jealousy wherewith God is jealous for His own glory. (ENOT)

This can be difficult because, as verse 10 admits, God's **people** are **scattered** and often feel alone. It is in this loneliness that faithful waiting becomes all the more difficult and all the more important. The result of waiting for the Lord is the ability to work together **shoulder to shoulder** (v. 9) in service to God.

WORDS FROM WESLEY

Zephaniah 3:10

My dispersed—The praying remnant of the scattered Jews shall return to their own land, and bring themselves an offering unto the Lord. (ENOT)

No Shame on That Day (Zeph. 3:11–15)

Beginning with verse 11, the rest of this passage reads much like a song. This is all the more interesting with the references to singing in verses 14 and 17. Singing is a common response in the Old Testament to salvation. Indeed, the **city**, the community, **will not be put to shame** (v. 11) on the day of the Lord because He will save them by removing the cause of their sin from their midst.

It is important to note that the **you** in verse 11 is plural. Again, Zephaniah was concerned with the kingdom as a whole. Individuals who caused sin to come upon the community were to be removed. Our current heightened sense of individualism can be bothered by this theme, yet it is the very importance of each individual that necessitates this tactic. Each person's spirituality directly affects the spiritual condition of the entire community (or church).

The continual issue is pride, which is in contrast with the fear of the Lord. Throughout the Old Testament, pride is the cause for the scattering of the people.

God's answer was to leave **the meek and humble, who trust in the name of the LORD** (v. 12) within the city. It is the fact that they trusted in the name of the Lord that made them meek and humble. This is an important point. Meekness and humility do not guarantee that a person will trust in the Lord. However, trust in the Lord does guarantee meekness and humility because trusting in the Lord produces meekness and humility.

Verse 13 takes up again the issue of purified lips. The definition of doing **no wrong** in this verse is speaking **no lies** and having no **deceit . . . in their mouths**. Notice the Hebrew affinity for parallelism. What we consider redundant, the Hebrew mind found necessary. Therefore, the same subjects are taken up again and again in order to sear the teaching in the mind.

Furthermore, verse 13 connects lying and deceit to starvation, sleeplessness, and fear. Lying and deceit are products of pride.

Pride leads people away from the Lord. Whoever is separated from the Lord is subject to maltreatment. That is the logic. It is communicated, not in propositions, but in poetic verse.

The singing in verse 15 has the impression of the present. Israel was to sing now, in the hope of the day of the Lord for which they were waiting. Even though it had not occurred yet, the fact that God issued the decree that it would come gave the people the ability to celebrate as if it had happened, This sense of celebrating what has yet to occur transferred into Christian worship in reference to the return of Christ and the resurrection of the dead.

Verse 15 assured the people that the true **King of Israel** is always with the faithful, even when the earthly king leads them astray. In a time when people were totally dependent upon their king and his relationship with other kings for their safety, this was a potent promise.

WORDS FROM WESLEY

Zephaniah 3:15

Taken away—Abolished, and put an end to the judgments thy sins brought upon thee. *Thine enemy*—The Babylonian. *Is in the midst*—He is returned to redeem and govern thee. *Any more*—While thy carriage is as becomes my presence with thee, thou shalt neither fear, nor feel the like evils. (ENOT)

No Fear on That Day (Zeph. 3:16–18)

The absence of fear is so replete that the enemies of Israel were the comforters. **They** in verse 16, who were saying, **"Do not fear . . . the Lord your God is with you"** (vv. 16–17), were their enemies referenced in verse 15!

Verse 17 is a complete reversal of God's wrath. Because of God's own salvation that He brought to the people, He rejoiced over them. This theme is taken up in Hebrews 2:11 and 11:16.

Probably the clearest New Testament example of this theme is Revelation 21:3–4. "And I heard a loud voice from the throne saying, 'Now the dwelling of God is with men, and he will live with them. They will be his people, and God himself will be with them and be their God. He will wipe every tear from their eyes. There will be no more death or mourning or crying or pain, for the old order of things has passed away.'"

It is the passing of the "old order" that is referenced in Zephaniah 3:18. The alternate translation for the verse is, "I will gather you who mourn for the appointed feasts; your reproach is a burden to you." The law, as Paul said, was given so that our sin could be exposed. When the sin is removed, the law is taken away, because then it is only a painful memory of what we were—enemies to God in our minds. We tend to forget that salvation is for us. God saves us for His sake, however, He saves us so we can know sin no longer—neither the sin nor the burden of sin. This is indeed a new order with no fear.

"I Will" Is "I Am" in Action (Zeph. 3:19–20)

Though Jesus quoted from Isaiah in Luke 4:18–19, the same theme could have been taken from Zephaniah 3:19: **At that time I will deal with all who oppressed you; I will rescue the lame and gather those who have been scattered. I will give them praise and honor in every land where they were put to shame.** Again, the context of Zephaniah's prophecy is like that of Isaiah. Relating hope to a scattered people, giving them solace that salvation is at hand.

The repetition of **I will** throughout Zephaniah 3:19–20 is a literary technique designed to produce that hope. We tend to read it in terms of time—future. The Hebrews would read it in terms of certainty. God will act. We must wait on Him. When He acts, it is definitive. We must not miss it. Jesus told many parables about waiting and being prepared.

The culminating "I will" is at the end of verse 20, **when I restore your fortunes before your very eyes.** The hope of seeing God's salvation was as old as Job: "I myself will see him with my own eyes—I, and not another. How my heart yearns within me!" (19:27). Again it is referenced with Jesus when Simeon said, "For my eyes have seen your salvation, which you have prepared in the sight of all people, a light for revelation to the Gentiles and for glory to your people Israel" (Luke 2:30–32).

This hope is not wishful thinking or an ethereal transcendence, but a real, tangible, physical salvation. It is true that it will be manifested in God's time, hence the repetition of **at that time** (Zeph. 3:19–20); but this again is not to put salvation in the dim light of the future. It is to put us on active watch in the present so we may be ready to receive when He comes.

WORDS FROM WESLEY

Zephaniah 3:20

A praise—So the universal church of the first-born will be, in the great day. And then the Israel of God be made a name and a praise to all eternity. (ENOT)

DISCUSSION

Discuss the most effective way for nations to enforce international laws on other nations: diplomacy, embargoes, military action, etc.

1. How does God enforce His will on rogue countries and individuals?

2. What are "purified lips"? Why would they be important to God?

3. What image comes to mind when you think of people calling on God together and serving Him "shoulder to shoulder"? Have you seen Christians doing this? How and when?

4. When do you think the scattered people of God will finally be united in worshiping Him?

5. God readily forgives past sins, but what will be done to safeguard the future of His holy hill?

6. How would you describe your nation—as prideful and haughty or as humble and meek? Which description best fits your church? You?

7. Verse 17 records that God "will take great delight in you, he will quiet you with his love, he will rejoice over you with singing." Think about that promise as applying to you personally. What effect does that thought have on you?

PRAYER

Father, we find comfort and strength in Your redemptive love and promise to care for us. Your judgment against sin is sure and awful. We will be eternally grateful to escape Your wrath because of the forgiveness that is ours in Christ. However, our hearts break when we think of those we love who are lost in their sins. Use us to help them escape Your punishment of sin.

10

FIRST THINGS FIRST

Haggai 1:1–15

We must give God first place in our lives.

Building anything can be an inspiring event. Congregations, for example, often experience an upswing in growth and momentum when breaking ground for a new facility. People are drawn to the energy of the new enterprise. Even when there are challenges or setbacks — perhaps especially then — people will come together to achieve something greater than themselves. Often, though, that momentum can wane, and those who were enthusiastic for the larger goal become self-absorbed and interested in advancing themselves, not the group goal.

This shift to selfishness was observed by Haggai as the former exiles returned from their captivity in Babylon to begin rebuild Jerusalem. They started well by rebuilding the foundation of the temple. Unfortunately, they changed course and became self-absorbed instead of self-sacrificing until the prophet Haggai came with his message from the Lord. This study calls us to examine our motives and be sure that we are truly serving God and not ourselves.

COMMENTARY

Haggai is one of the most precisely dated books of the Old Testament. Verse 1 starts the book by saying, "In the second year of King Darius, on the first day of the sixth month, the word of the LORD came through the prophet Haggai." This translates into August 29, 520 BC. The message of Haggai was given by God to the prophet over the following four months.

The central message of the book has to do with the rebuilding of the temple in Jerusalem. Seventy-seven years before Haggai was written, Babylon invaded Jerusalem and partially destroyed Solomon's temple. Eleven years later, there was a second invasion, and the whole city was razed. This was the beginning of the Babylonian exile. At this time, a second round of deportations ensued. Some of the Old Testament books were written during this time of exile.

Much of the spiritual life of Israel was tied to the land that God had given them through Abraham. Although life in Babylon was relatively easy, as far as captivity goes, being in exile was seen as a hardship. The people of God wanted to get back to their country.

There were a number of times when a group of Jewish people returned from Babylon to Jerusalem. Zerubbabel was the governor of Jerusalem. He led the first group of exiles back to Jerusalem in 536 BC (1:1; Ezra 3:2). This was an incredible miracle. The country that had captured the people of God was allowing them to return to their homeland. The book of Haggai was written to Zerubbabel and through him to the people of God, sixteen years after this return.

God's Issue (Hag. 1:1–4)

When the people of God returned, they found the city in ruins. Although one of the primary missions given to them was the reconstruction of the temple (Ezra 1), the first thing they did was rebuild their houses, typically out of stone and plaster, the most common building material of the day.

This was not problematic; God understood that they needed places to live. But now the people had been back in their own land for sixteen years. Not only had they rebuilt their houses; now they had paneled their houses. Paneling was usually done in palaces; thus it was a sign of luxury.

God's issue with the people was that they were fixated on their own luxury in their own house and that they had left God's house in ruins (Hag. 1:4). God's house, the temple, was the center of worship, the place where sacrifices were made. It was the place that contained the ark of the covenant, the place where people went to seek out the presence of God. It was the center of worship. God's issue was that the people were pampering themselves and ignoring Him.

Now, the people had some reasonable excuses. The first excuse was that it was politically risky to rebuild the temple. Jerusalem had many enemies, many of whom did not want to see the temple rebuilt. Political lobbying had even prohibited the rebuilding of temple for a time (see Ezra 4:4–5).

By the time we get to Haggai, Darius was the king of Persia and the legal opposition had been removed. But even now the people would not rebuild the temple. They said, **"The time has not yet come for the LORD's house to be built"** (Hag. 1:2). They had been indulging themselves, the opposition against the building had died down somewhat, but still they were saying it was not the right time. They wanted to procrastinate.

The People's Issue (Hag. 1:5–7)

The people were leading thoughtless lives. Five times throughout the book of Haggai the people are commanded, **"Give careful thought to your ways"** (vv. 5, 7; 2:15, 18 [twice]). If the people would have thought about it, they would have known something was wrong. As it was, they were living shallow lives, pampering themselves, without seeing the problem. God had to speak directly into their situation.

God pointed out to these people what they would have seen if they would have looked for themselves: **"You have planted much, but have harvested little. You eat, but never have enough. You drink, but never have your fill. You put on clothes, but are not warm. You earn wages, only to put them in a purse with holes in it"** (1:6).

WORDS FROM WESLEY

Haggai 1:6

Have not enough — But what you eat doth not nourish or satisfy you. *Are not filled* — Your water quenches not your thirst, your wine does not revive your spirit. *None warm* — You have no comfort therein. *With holes* — Loses all his labour. (ENOT)

There is a sense in which these people never seem to be able to get enough. They were not starving, but they were not satisfied either. They had the essentials, but they didn't seem to have what they needed. They worked hard but had little to show for it.

Had these people known the Torah, and had they given careful thought to what was happening to them, they would have been able to define this phenomenon. What was happening is exactly what one would expect as the people of God, if the blessing of God was removed from your life. It is not that they had cursed themselves by being involved in idol worship or some other such blasphemy. It was just that the blessing of God was not there.

In our time, prophecy is often pitted against thinking. Some would say that if we are going to listen to God then we need to give up thinking for ourselves. There are others who would say that if we would just think, then we wouldn't have to listen to God. In this passage, the people were listening to God and they were being told to think.

God's Solution (Hag. 1:8–11)

God told His people to reorder their priorities. He let them know that the lack of blessing was due to their being busy with their own houses while His temple was in ruins (v. 9). God's expectation was that they would **go up into the mountains** and gather material to **build** a place where He could **be honored** (v. 8).

The application of this principle has to be carefully nuanced in our busy church world. The temple was the center of worship; worship is a priority. It was a center of sacrifice; confession, humility, and holiness are priorities. It was a center of community; love is a priority. It was the place to pray; prayer is a priority. It was the place to encounter the presence of God and commune with God; these are priorities. Becoming busy in our church world may or may not be part of making these priorities part of our lives.

WORDS FROM WESLEY

Haggai 1:7

O may I call my ways to mind,
My past unfaithfulness,
And, when by Thee afflicted, find
The cause of my distress!
O may I for Thine absence mourn,
Till Thou my guilt remove,
And fill my heart by Thy return
With perfect peace and love! (PW, vol. 10, 109)

A Christian life that is not prioritized around God will, over time, see the blessing of God diminished. He or she will sense this holy dissatisfaction. Life will move along as it should, but it will not feel as fulfilling as it should.

God was very clear about what was happening to His people. **"You expected much, but see, it turned out to be little. What you brought home, I blew away. . . . Because of you the heavens have withheld their dew and the earth its crops. I called for a drought on the fields and the mountains, on the grain, the new wine, the oil and whatever the ground produces, on men and cattle, and on the labor of your hands"** (vv. 9–11).

Notice how active God was in this process. This dissatisfaction came straight from His hands. The judgments of God are always for the purpose of redemption. God did not withhold His blessing out of spite or meanness. God knew the people would be in trouble if they went much longer without centering their community around the worship of God. They would move inevitably from their current shallow concern for themselves to idolatry. Idolatry inevitably moves toward baser evils. This kind of evil brings darkness and death. God saw the direction His people were headed and called them back.

The People's Response (Hag. 1:12–15)

The people obeyed the voice of the LORD their God (v. 12). The people could have chosen a number of responses. They could have chosen to continue to procrastinate. They could have said, "Yes, we know we need to build the temple, and we will — sometime." But they didn't put it off; they obeyed.

Often when people don't like the message, they call into question the character of the messenger. But these people did not call Haggai a false prophet because they knew **the LORD their God had sent him** (v. 12).

God responded to the people's obedience by saying, **"I am with you"** (v. 13). In this simple statement was all the assurance they needed. They would be reminded of God's promise to Moses: "My Presence will go with you" (Ex. 33:14). They would understand that that the blessing of God comes with the presence of God.

By speaking that simple phrase "I am with you," God spoke into all the issues the people had been experiencing. That sense of dissatisfaction was about to pass. The people were about to be satisfied. The time of spiritual restlessness and lack of supply had come to an end because the people of God were promised the presence of God. This did not mean life would be easy or without challenges. The people of God, however, would now know the satisfaction of God.

It is hard to underestimate the power of the presence of God in the Old Testament. With the presence of God came blessing, strength, guidance, protection, and provision. The temple was supposed to be the place to find the presence of God. In this case, however, the presence of God came with obedience to God. Obedience is often the key to unlock the presence of God.

Obedience usually results in a change of behavior. The word of the Lord came to Haggai on the "first day of the sixth month" (Hag. 1:1). Work began on the temple **on the twenty-fourth day of the sixth month** (v. 15). It often takes time to hear the word, process what has been said, and then implement what has been commanded. Often what happens is that people hear the Word of God and are stirred to action. Motivation, however, seems to be lost in the time it takes to implement what is being called for. People often tend to slip back into a procrastination mode. These people in Haggai are to be commended for following through on their commitment.

●

WORDS FROM WESLEY

Haggai 1:15

The Lord of hosts—By which name He delights to be known among the returned captives; and it was a name best suited to their present state, compassed on all hands with enemies. (ENOT)

DISCUSSION

Share your last significant life change and what motivated you to make it.

1. After returning from exile, rebuilding the temple was begun only to be abandoned for fifteen years. When have you seen God's work sit idle while other projects progressed?

2. When faced with an overwhelming task, how do you set priorities?

3. How does God's list of things to consider in verse 6 help us to evaluate our ways?

4. What is the danger of saying, "It is not time yet" if God is saying, "It's time"?

5. What was the reason God gave for building His house? Would those be the same reasons church building committees use today? What other reasons are given?

6. Although this is a time-specific situation, what general principles can be taken from this Scripture passage?

7. The people recognized that Haggai was the Lord's messenger and all the people agreed. If people are not in agreement, how can they know who speaks on behalf of the Lord?

8. What response did the people's obedience receive from God? Is that response worth our obedience?

PRAYER

Father, we declare You to be the supreme object of our worship. Everything else takes a lesser place in our love and commitment. Teach us to order our lives so that we never allow anything to crowd You out or to diminish our love toward You.

11

LISTEN FOR GOD'S SIGNAL

Zechariah 9:16—10:12

When we respond to God's call, He strengthens us.

The book of Zechariah is like a science fiction thriller in which the time element is a bit confused. We see glimpses of the present, past, and future, and it can take a bit of doing to determine which scenes are flashbacks and which represent the current day.

This book, however, delivers a powerful message about the faithfulness of God. In our lives — as in this prophecy — the same God stands as Lord over the past, present, and future. Regardless of the order in which we choose to tell the story, the ending is always the same: A faithful God will redeem His faithful people.

Zechariah's name means "whom the Lord remembers," and this study emphasizes that theme — the long and sure memory of God. Regardless of the current circumstances and regardless of any trouble that may come in the future, God is sure to remember His people and to restore their fortunes.

COMMENTARY

Zechariah was a prophet who came from a priestly family like Jeremiah and Ezekiel, but unlike Amos. Zechariah was born in Babylon during the exile and became an important figure in the rebuilding of the temple when the Israelites returned to Jerusalem in 537 BC. He prophesied at the same time as Haggai, but for much longer. It is estimated that Zechariah's ministry lasted until the reign of the Babylonian king Artaxerxes I (465–424 BC).

The passage for this study is in the section of judgment and salvation oracles and qualifies as the latter. In this passage, the meaning of Zechariah's name is particularly appropriate to the context of his message. Not only does God remember, but Zechariah wanted the people, especially the leaders, to remember both the punishments (exiles) and salvations (returns, coming out) of the past. It is in these that hope for the future is found and secured.

Salvation Is Beautiful (Zech. 9:16–17)

We rarely consider this aspect of salvation—that the saved are **beautiful** (v. 17). They sparkle. They are **attractive** (v. 17). Especially in the Old Testament, salvation is expressly physical. One reason was the physical insecurity of the times. Poverty, hardship, and even slavery were constant threats.

WORDS FROM WESLEY

Zechariah 9:17

How great Thy beauty who can tell,
Or all Thy loveliness explore!
Their face the dazzled seraphs veil,
And prostrate at Thy throne adore:
Thy goodness all their thoughts transcends:
But man, his God's supreme delight,
Fill'd with Thy love, he comprehends
The length, and breadth, and depth, and height! (PW, vol. 10, 120)

In this age, the security of the people resided in the king. This part of the prophecy declares God to be the King who will bring prosperity, wealth, and safety. So thorough will this be that the people themselves will be the **jewels** of His **crown** (v. 16). Their fields and vineyards will produce enough to nourish them to full health. Their skin will glow. Their hair and nails will be healthy. Their fertility will be vigorous and celebrated.

The beauty of God is reflected in the beauty of His people who are called by His name into the salvation of His righteousness. God invests himself in the people whom He saves. This investment pays dividends in beauty.

Maybe this imagery would call the garden of Eden to mind, where everything was pristine and God looked upon what He had created and called it good. These verses definitely echo Ezekiel 16:14: "And your fame spread among the nations on account of your beauty, because the splendor I had given you made your beauty perfect, declares the Sovereign LORD." Even amid harsh condemnation, Isaiah relates beauty with the remaining hope of salvation: "In that day the Branch of the LORD will be beautiful and glorious, and the fruit of the land will be the pride and glory of the survivors in Israel" (4:2).

WORDS FROM WESLEY
Zechariah 9:17

His goodness—Infinite goodness is the fountain of all the good done for this people. *His beauty*—How wonderful the beauty of Divine Providence in Israel's deliverance and salvation? *Corn*—Plentiful harvests shall make the young men cheerful in sowing, reaping, and eating the fruits thereof. *New wine*—There shall be such plenty of wine, that all, young and old shall be cheered with it. (ENOT)

Living God versus Idols and False Prophets (Zech. 10:1–3)

Ask the LORD for rain in the springtime; it is the LORD who makes the storm clouds (v. 1). Zechariah reminded the people that God is the source of life. In an agricultural society, the most important natural resource is water. Many ancient kings elevated themselves to that status by convincing the people that they could control either the rain or the floodwaters, or both, especially in Egypt.

Much of the religious debate of the times was over which deity brought rain and under what conditions. The second half of verse 1 places the God of Israel as the generous God of all humankind. God does not show partiality with the rain and the plants that it feeds. **He gives showers of rain to men, and plants of the field to everyone** (v. 1).

From here Zechariah moved to idols and false prophets. It is interesting that the **idols** are said to **speak deceit** (v. 2). This is not a concession to the ability of idols. The author used "speaking idols" in parallel with **diviners** who **see visions that lie** (v. 2). This is yet another example of the Hebrew's passion for parallelism. They found it more forceful to think and teach in couplets and triplets than in singular sequential logic.

Zechariah also used "lying idols" to highlight the sin and responsibility of the false prophets. Notice the idols lie, but the diviners see false visions, proclaim false dreams, and give empty comfort. This is to say that the sin of the people for following idols is outweighed by the sin of the priests and prophets who encourage it for their own security and wealth.

The result is a wandering and aimless people, even in the midst of supposed worldly safety and security. People in this condition are ultimately like unprotected sheep, vulnerable to the elements and attack from multiple predators. Thus verse 3 declares that God's **anger burns against the shepherds**, and He **will punish the leaders**. It appears the punishment is removal from office and having God himself take over.

The Power of Salvation (Zech. 10:3–5)

God's care is directly related to power as compared to the powerlessness of the false prophets. God is introduced in verse 3 as **the LORD Almighty**. God's power is part of His care. His salvation comes from His love, and it comes in power. Remember Zephaniah 3:17: "The LORD your God is with you, he is mighty to save. He will take great delight in you, he will quiet you with his love, he will rejoice over you with singing." Because of this, Judah would raise her head like a mighty battle horse.

This pride and strength will cover every aspect of life. Zechariah 10:4 addresses the four primary conditions of ancient life: settled, wandering, war, and peace. **From Judah will come the cornerstone** is a reference to building cities and fortifications. The **tent peg** references wandering or migrating. In the ancient world, there were constant conflicts between settled and unsettled peoples. Settled people considered unsettled people barbaric. Unsettled people considered settled people weak. **From . . . the battle bow** obviously references war. **Every ruler** is a not-so-obvious reference to peace. Although imperialism was growing in Zechariah's time, most rulers were judged not by their expansion through war, but by their ability to procure peace and stability by which commercial wealth flourished.

The Joy of Salvation (Zech. 10:6–7)

When David repented of his sin, he said, "Have mercy on me, O God, according to your unfailing love; according to your great compassion blot out my transgressions. . . . Restore to me the joy of your salvation and grant me a willing spirit, to sustain me" (Ps. 51:1, 12). In this request from David we find God's promise in Zechariah 10:6–7.

The reason **Judah**, **Joseph**, and the **Ephraimites** (vv. 6–7) are mentioned is not because of their historical situation, but because of the theological implications of their names. In Genesis 29:35, Leah gave her fourth son the name Judah because it was a praise to the Lord. In Genesis 30:23, Rachel said, "God has taken away my disgrace," and named her son Joseph because it means "may he add." In Genesis 41:52, Joseph named his son Ephraim "because God has made me fruitful in the land of my suffering." Mentioning these names is the Hebrew's poetic way of saying, "God will increase our praise, add to us strength and health, and multiply us even in the midst of hard circumstances."

WORDS FROM WESLEY

Zechariah 10:6

Of Joseph—The remnant of the kingdom of Israel, the residue of the ten tribes. *To place them*—To settle them in their own land, and in their own cities. (ENOT)

The Return of Salvation (Zech. 10:8–10)

Since the old covenant was indivisibly associated with the Promised Land, throughout the Old Testament condemnation was associated with exile, and salvation with return. God calling and gathering are common motifs for salvation in the Old Testament. The reference to **as numerous as before** (v. 8) is not only a call to remember (probably) their numbers during the unified kingdom under David and Solomon, but also a reference to God's promise to Abraham: "I will surely bless you and make your descendants as numerous as the stars in the sky and as the sand on the seashore" (Gen. 22:17).

On many occasions in the Old Testament, children are included in both the blessings and punishments placed on the people. The ancient people were highly communal in their worldview. Nothing happened to an individual without implications, at least, and direct consequence, at most, for the community as a whole.

Zechariah 10:10 uses two bygone foes to situate both the present and future hope. **Egypt** was the power from whom the Israelites originally escaped. **Assyria** had conquered the northern kingdom around 720 BC. These exiles had never returned. For the prophecy to include them shows the far-reaching cosmic reordering that Zechariah had in mind. At the time of the prophecy, both Egypt and Assyria had passed as world powers and Babylon was in power. The idea is that Babylon would go the same way the other two had.

Also, the mention of **Lebanon** (v. 10) continues the theme of beauty, thus a return to beauty. The Israelites became proud of their beauty, according to Ezekiel 16:15, and this was the point of God's punishment in Ezekiel 28:7: "I am going to bring foreigners against you, the most ruthless of nations; they will draw their swords against your beauty and wisdom and pierce your shining splendor." However, bringing them back to Lebanon was bringing them back to beauty. Ezekiel 31:7–8 describes Lebanon as "majestic in beauty, with its spreading boughs, for its roots went down to abundant waters. The cedars in the garden of God could not rival it, nor could the pine trees equal its boughs, nor could the plane trees compare with its branches—no tree in the garden of God could match its beauty."

The Righteous Will Overcome (Zech. 10:11–12)

Verse 11 continues the concept of the fall of Israel's enemies by remembering the past victories. The sea was always a source and symbol of chaos for the Israelites. Though they had some naval experience, by and large they were not a seagoing people and regarded the sea as an uncontrollable force, usually destructive.

Egypt rose to power primarily because of the Nile. Its flood pattern was regular and predictable. Therefore crops could be easily and well irrigated. It seemed like an endless resource. That God would dry up the Nile was a part of the prophetic tradition inherited by Zechariah. Ezekiel 30:12 states, "I will dry up the streams of the Nile and sell the land to evil men." Isaiah 19:5, 7 prophesies concerning Egypt, "The waters of the river will dry up and the riverbed will be parched and dry . . . also the plants along the Nile, at the mouth of the river. Every sown field along the Nile will become parched, will blow away and be no more."

So we come full circle, back to the beginning of the prophecy that declared God "gives showers of rain to men and plants of the field to everyone." The Nile was Egypt's security. Assyria boasted in her strength. Instead of being the light that shone in the darkness, Israel regularly melded with the beliefs of those whom they felt were stronger and wealthier. By strengthening **them in the LORD**, and by having them walk **in his name** (Zech. 10:12), God is offering hope, not only to Israel, but to the entire world.

WORDS FROM WESLEY

Zechariah 10:12

Walk up and down—Shall manage all their affairs. *In his name*—By power and wisdom given from above, to the glory of our God, and our Redeemer. (ENOT)

DISCUSSION

Share what the most beautiful and valuable thing you own is.

1. From this Scripture passage, we see that God values His people, yet they are in a sad state. Why is that?

2. What is a "false shepherd"? Who were the false shepherds back then? Who are false shepherds today?

3. Why would God be so angry with false shepherds? Do you think He is more angry at them than others who do wrong? Why or why not?

4. To whom do you believe God was referring in 10:4?

5. In what ways does Jesus fit the image of the cornerstone? A tent peg? A battle bow? A ruler?

6. After the sheep of Israel and return to God's "flock," Zechariah wrote, "I will restore them because I have compassion on them. They will be as though I had not rejected them, for I am the LORD their God" (v. 6). List several conclusions you could draw from this about God's forgiveness.

7. What situations have you seen God restore in the past? Do you believe God has the power to restore *any* situation?

8. In what ways does God strengthen His flock?

PRAYER

Father, we know Jesus as the Good Shepherd who knows His sheep and calls them by name. He is the source of our salvation, strength, and joy. Thank You for restoring in us what sin destroyed.

SERVING GOD WHOLEHEARTEDLY

Malachi 3:6–18

God desires that we devote our lives entirely to Him.

Some things are either all or nothing. It is impossible to be a "little bit" pregnant. A spouse cannot be "mostly" faithful. There is no such thing as a "half-truth." While it may be possible to be in "semiretirement," there's no way to be "sort of" consecrated to God. You either are fully devoted to Him or you are not.

Malachi, the last and perhaps most fiery of the Old Testament preachers, emphasized that point to the complacent people of God. Because they believed they were holy as a matter of national identity, the prophet challenged them to see that holiness is pervasive—it must infiltrate every area of life and behavior. In the end, it will produce a people—and individuals—who are unmistakably different from those around them.

This study calls us to a full, rich relationship with God. It points out the consequence of failure to serve God wholeheartedly, calls for change, and makes clear what the changes involve. Let it become your opportunity to repent, to exercise faithful stewardship, and to trust God's purpose and plans for your life.

COMMENTARY

Malachi and the Old Testament end with these words: "Remember the law of my servant Moses, the decrees and laws I gave him at Horeb for all Israel. See, I will send you the prophet Elijah before that great and dreadful day of the LORD comes. He will turn the hearts of the fathers to their children, and the hearts of the children to their fathers; or else I will come and strike the land with a curse" (4:4–6). Then came a period of some four hundred years without a prophet's voice in Israel. Certainly there remained many devout people calling for righteousness during the time between the testaments.

Malachi, as the last Old Testament prophet, ended with an exhortation and a promise. He exhorted the Jews to remember the law of Moses and proclaimed the prophecy of a future prophet to come before the great day of the Lord. The Jews in Jesus' day were still looking for the fulfillment of Malachi's prophecy when Jesus identified John the Baptist as the promised Elijah who was to come (Matt. 11:11–14).

Little is known of Malachi, the latest of the Old Testament prophets. His name means "my messenger," and some scholars have suggested that "Malachi" may be a description of the prophet rather than a proper name. Dating for the prophet is also uncertain. Malachi condemns several sins of the people that are also condemned by Nehemiah, so some scholars surmise that he may have been a contemporary of Nehemiah. If so, that would place Malachi's prophecy in the latter half of the fifth century BC. The *NIV Study Bible* places Nehemiah's two terms as governor as beginning in 445 BC and ending sometime prior to 407 BC.

Malachi's question-and-answer style is distinctive. Several times in this short prophecy he recorded a statement from the Lord, followed by a question from the people related to the statement. Then he gave the Lord's responses (1:2, 6–7; 2:14, 17; 3:7–8, 13). Several more questions from the Lord also add to the framework of the oracle.

Malachi also used several striking word pictures to focus the attention of his audience: (1) the priests sniff at the sacrifices (1:12–13); (2) offal from the sacrifices will be smeared on the faces of the priests (2:3); (3) the Levites will be refined as silver (3:3); and (4) the evildoers will burn as stubble, but the Sun of

Righteousness will rise for those who revere God's name (4:1–2). This short book is unique.

A century earlier the Jews had returned from exile. Cyrus followed a benevolent policy that allowed them to return from Babylon to Israel and Jerusalem. Under the first governor, Zerubbabel, the prophets Haggai and Zechariah encouraged the people, and the temple had been rebuilt. The sacrificial system had also been restored. Some decades later, Ezra the priest had led more exiles as they returned. Ezra took steps to revive the spirits of the people and to restore zeal for their religious practices. About the same time, Nehemiah was appointed governor, and he led the people in rebuilding the wall of Jerusalem. Progress in restoring the nation had been made, but circumstances for the returned exiles remained quite discouraging. They were a small nation on the edge of the huge Persian Empire. The promised Messiah had not yet appeared. Temple worship was halfhearted. The economy was sluggish, and most of the people were poor, barely eking out a living. Probably for many of the Jews it seemed like God had forgotten His chosen people.

This is the setting in which Malachi proclaimed an oracle from the Lord. Though the people might be discouraged and halfhearted in their worship, Malachi urged them to be faithful. He proclaimed God's promise anew—the day of the Lord was coming.

Faithful God (Mal. 3:6–7)

"I the LORD do not change. So you, O descendants of Jacob, are not destroyed. Ever since the time of your forefathers you have turned away from my decrees and have not kept them. Return to me, and I will return to you," says the LORD Almighty (vv. 6–7).

The Jews who had returned to Israel were not faithful in following the law of Moses. Malachi had already rebuked them for offering blemished sacrifices (1:6–14). He rebuked priests for unfaithfulness (2:1–9). Divorce apparently was common among them, and Malachi rebuked Judah because husbands were being unfaithful to their wives (2:10–16). Considering their many sins, the Jews deserved to be destroyed. But God was faithful to them, and they were spared. Malachi warned them that they were following the ways of their forefathers. Like their forefathers, they were unfaithful, ignoring God's decrees.

God's faithfulness stood in striking contrast to the Jews' unfaithfulness. God spoke through Malachi, urging them to returned to the Lord. If they returned to Him, He would return to them. Once again this illustrates God's gracious pattern with humankind. In spite of the Jews' sinfulness, God remained faithful. The wonderful truth is that God accepts all who will return to Him.

WORDS FROM WESLEY
Malachi 3:6

I change not—I have an unchangeable hatred to sin: and my long suffering also changeth not, therefore you are not consumed in your sins. *Not consumed*—God is the same in His wisdom to order the rewards of good and bad in the fittest season, therefore neither the one nor the other are consumed, but preserved to the season appointed of God. (ENOT)

Robbing God (Mal. 3:7–10)

"But you ask, 'How are we to return?' Will a man rob God? Yet you rob me. But you ask, 'How do we rob you?' In tithes and offerings. You are under a curse—the whole nation of you—because you are robbing me. Bring the whole tithe into the storehouse, that there may be food in my house. Test me in this," says the LORD Almighty (vv. 7–10).

In this passage, Malachi's question-and-answer style is evident. God had said for the people to return to Him. The people then asked, **"How are we to return?"** The answer came that they were robbing God. The people then asked, **"How do we rob you?"** God answered, **"In tithes and offerings."** They were under a curse because of their failure. They had not presented their tithes and offerings to the Lord. There was not enough grain and other produce to provide for God's house. Note that Malachi had already rebuked the priests. Apparently the people were at fault also because they had not adequately provided for the priests.

It is not hard to understand the people's failure to pay tithes to the priests who were guilty of corrupt behavior. But Malachi made it clear that failure to pay tithes still was not a legitimate option for them. Failure to pay tithes and offerings was robbing God, not the priests. The application for today seems obvious.

WORDS FROM WESLEY
Malachi 3:10

Bring ye—Make a punctual and full payment of all tithes; about this did Nehemiah contend with the rulers, and made them comply, and then all Judah obeyed and did the like (Neh. 13:10–13). *To the store-house*—This was one or more large rooms, built on purpose for this use. *That there may be meat*—For the priests and Levites to live upon. *Prove me*—Make the experiment. *The windows of heaven*—A kind of proverbial speech, to express great abundance. *A blessing*—First of rain to water the earth, next a blessing of corn, wine and oil, and all other products of the earth. (ENOT)

Testing God (Mal. 3:10–12)

God then challenged them to test Him. If they would **bring the whole tithe into the storehouse**, they would be blessed. **See if I will not throw open the floodgates of heaven and pour out so much blessing that you will not have room enough for it. I will prevent pests from devouring your crops, and the vines in your fields will not cast their fruit** (vv. 10–11). The blessing and provision will be so great that **then all the nations will call you blessed, for yours will be a delightful land** (v. 12). A few decades earlier, the prophet Haggai had given an opposite message. Haggai urged the Jews to proceed with rebuilding the temple and gave God's message that "because of you the heavens have withheld their dew and the earth its crops. I called for a drought on the fields and the mountains, on the grain, the new wine, the oil and whatever the ground produces, on men and cattle, and on the labor of your hands" (Hag. 1:10–11). We may wonder if God gives or withholds blessing today, but the testimonies that God blesses those who are faithful in their support of His work are many.

WORDS FROM WESLEY
Malachi 3:10

All nations—All that are about you. *A delightsome land*—The revival of religion in a land, will make it delightsome, both to God, and to all good men (ENOT)

Forgetting God (Mal. 3:13–15)

"You have said harsh things against me," says the LORD. "Yet you ask, 'What have we said against you?' You have said, 'It is futile to serve God. What did we gain by carrying out his requirements and going about like mourners before the LORD Almighty? But now we call the arrogant blessed. Certainly the evildoers prosper, and even those who challenge God escape'" (vv. 13–15).

Malachi recorded another accusation from God against the people, and again they replied with a question. They had said false things about the Lord, nevertheless they feigned innocence. In circumstances that seem discouraging, they gave up on serving the Lord. Their religion became meaningless to them. Wearing sackcloth and ashes as mourners appeared to bring no benefit. In their discouragement, the people gave up on the promises of God. They forgot His miraculous power that had delivered them time and again. Most recently they had been delivered from the exile in Babylon. God knew their hearts and still remained faithful to them, but they had to return to Him.

Remembering God (Mal. 3:16)

Then those who feared the LORD talked with each other, and the LORD listened and heard. A scroll of remembrance was written in his presence concerning those who feared the LORD and honored his name (v. 16).

A return to the Lord began with those faithful Jews who feared the Lord. They communicated with each other to give and get mutual support, and they acknowledged their dependence on the divine favor. The Lord listened to their conversation as well. To seal their devotion to the Lord they put in writing **a scroll of remembrance.** This may have been a list of those who heeded Malachi's exhortations and agreed to obey God's decrees, or it may have been a record of God's faithfulness. They were returning to the Lord and were honoring His name. Whenever people return to God and honor His name, He hears. And He returns to them. God was waiting for such people in Malachi's day. Today God still waits for people to return. His promise remains: "Return to me, and I will return to you" (3:7).

Gracious God (Mal. 3:17–18)

"They will be mine," says the LORD Almighty, "in the day when I make up my treasured possession. I will spare them, just as in compassion a man spares his son who serves him. And you will again see the distinction between the righteous and the wicked, between those who serve God and those who do not" (vv. 17–18).

For all those who returned to the Lord, there was a special promise of His blessing. They would be part of His **treasured possession**. He would spare them as a father spares his sons, showing them compassion. He would bless them so that the righteous (and someday the unrighteous) would know it is not futile to serve God. The distinction between the righteous who serve God and the wicked who ignore God would become obvious for all to see. Now, as we ponder the inequities on earth, it may sometimes be hard to believe that it pays to serve God. But that will change, and in God's time it will be obvious.

WORDS FROM WESLEY

Malachi 3:17

Make up my jewels—This shall be fully made good in the last great day, and in heaven to eternal ages. *I will spare them*—In the mean time they shall be spared, pitied, preserved, and loved. (ENOT)

As Malachi continued in chapter 4, he went on to discuss the day of the Lord that is coming. For believers there is always an eschatological (end time) aspect to their hope that will be fulfilled only at the end of time in the day of the Lord. Our faith assures us even in the darkest circumstances that there is a day coming when God, who rules over all, will restore all things. As His **treasured possession**, the righteous will reign with Him. We are justified (made righteous) by faith, and we live in that hope. God is waiting for all who will return to Him. He wants everyone to participate in that hope.

DISCUSSION

Discuss if we are living in a time when we see no distinction in how the righteous and wicked live.

1. What does it meant to test God? Is testing God ever a good thing?

2. God made a conditional promise in 3:7. What was it? Can you think of other conditional promises God has made?

3. Malachi accused the Israelites of "robbing" God by withholding tithes and offerings. Do you think that's a fair assessment? Does it apply to you?

4. Because of their disobedience, God pronounced a judgment on the entire people. Does God still judge entire nations or other groups? Which ones? Or does He judge only individuals today?

5. God commanded them to "bring the whole tithe into the storehouse." What did He mean by "whole tithe"? Do you think this might apply to our calculations of tithe today—on net versus gross income, for example?

6. Have you ever thought, as people in those days did, that it was futile to serve God because evildoers seem to prosper while the righteous suffer?

PRAYER

Father, forgive us for the times we have drifted from You and given You less than our best. We turn our faces toward the Sun of Righteousness and rejoice in the healing He brings to our souls. May others see Jesus shining through our lives.

WORDS FROM WESLEY WORKS CITED

ENOT: Wesley, J. (1765). *Explanatory Notes upon the Old Testament* (Vol. 1–3). Bristol: William Pine.

PW: *The Poetical Works of John and Charles Wesley.* Edited by D. D. G. Osborn. 13 vols. London: Wesleyan-Methodist Conference Office, 1868.

WJW: *The Works of John Wesley.* Third Edition, Complete and Unabridged. 14 vols. London: Wesleyan Methodist Book Room, 1872.

OTHER BOOKS IN THE
WESLEY BIBLE STUDIES SERIES

Genesis
Exodus
Leviticus through Deuteronomy
Joshua through Ruth
1 Samuel through 2 Chronicles
Ezra through Esther
Job through Song of Songs
Isaiah
Jeremiah through Daniel
Hosea through Malachi
Matthew
Mark
Luke
John
Acts
Romans
1–2 Corinthians
Galatians through Colossians and Philemon
1–2 Thessalonians
1 Timothy through Titus
Hebrews
James
1–2 Peter and Jude
1–3 John
Revelation

Now Available in the Wesley Bible Studies Series

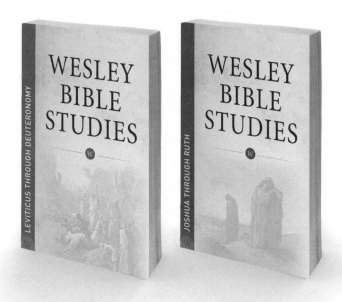

Each book in the Wesley Bible Studies series provides a thoughtful and powerful survey of key Scriptures in one or more biblical books. They combine accessible commentary from contemporary teachers, with relevantly highlighted direct quotes from the complete writings and life experiences of John Wesley, along with the poetry and hymns of his brother Charles. For each study, creative and engaging questions foster deeper fellowship and growth.

Leviticus through Deuteronomy
978-0-89827-858-3
978-0-89827-859-0 (e-book)

Joshua through Ruth
978-0-89827-860-6
978-0-89827-861-3 (e-book)

1.800.493.7539   wphstore.com